KIERKEGAARD'S CONCEPT OF DESPAIR

─────────── ꟽMP ───────────

PRINCETON MONOGRAPHS IN PHILOSOPHY

Harry G. Frankfurt, Series Editor

———————— •ꟼMP• ————————

The Princeton Monographs in Philosophy series offers short historical and systematic studies on a wide variety of philosophical topics.

Justice Is Conflict by Stuart Hampshire

Liberty Worth the Name by Gideon Yaffe

Self-Deception Unmasked by Alfred R. Mele

Public Goods, Private Goods by Raymond Geuss

Welfare and Rational Care by Stephen Darwall

A Defense of Hume on Miracles by Robert J. Fogelin

Kierkegaard's Concept of Despair by Michael Theunissen

KIERKEGAARD'S CONCEPT OF DESPAIR

Michael Theunissen

Translated by Barbara Harshav
and Helmut Illbruck

PRINCETON UNIVERSITY PRESS
PRINCETON AND OXFORD

First Published in Germany under the title *Der Begriff Verzweiflung:
Korrekturen an Kierkegaard* © Suhrkamp Verlag Frankfurt am Main 1993
English translation © 2005 by Princeton University Press
Published by Princeton University Press, 41 William Street,
Princeton, New Jersey 08540

In the United Kingdom: Princeton University Press,
3 Market Place, Woodstock, Oxfordshire OX20 1SY
All Rights Reserved

Library of Congress Cataloging-in-Publication Data
Theunissen, Michael.
[Begriff Verzweiflung. English]
Kierkegaard's concept of despair / Michael Theunissen ;
translated by Barbara Harshav and Helmut Illbruck
p.   cm.   (Princeton monographs in philosophy)
Includes bibliographical references and index.
ISBN 0-691-09558-2 (alk. paper)
1. Kierkegaard, Søren, 1813–1855. 2. Despair. 3. Sin. I. Title. II. Series.
B4377.T47313 2005
248—dc22   2004050383

British Library Cataloging-in-Publication Data is available

The publication of this work was supported
by a grant from the Goethe-Institut.

This book has been composed in Jason Text and Centaur

Printed on acid-free paper. ∞
pup.princeton.edu

Printed in the United States of America

1 3 5 7 9 10 8 6 4 2

Contents

Preface
vii

FIRST STUDY
The Existential Dialectical Basic Assumption
of Kierkegaard's Analysis of Despair
1

SECOND STUDY
On the Transcending Critique of Kierkegaard's
Analysis of Despair
34

SUMMARIZING CONCLUSION
Dialectic in *The Sickness unto Death*
105

Notes
121

Index
155

Preface

"Perhaps this book is not to be used at all." Thus Kierkegaard commented on the book discussed here, *The Sickness unto Death*, a few weeks after its completion in March and April of the revolutionary year of 1848.[1] The doubt about its usefulness refers not to its content but to its form. The religious writer who had chosen a rhymed prayer by Zinzendor as a motto asked himself in retrospect whether the book was not too "strict" to accomplish the purpose stated in its subtitle, and serve for "edification and conversion." The studies I present would have been loathsome for a man with such scruples. That is, they themselves neglect the rhetorical means he uses in no small measure, despite all strictness. The title, which refers to the *concept* of despair, alludes not only to Kierkegaard's treatise on anxiety, which he also feels is too speculative. The title also and mainly indicates that I would like to approach *The Sickness unto Death* analytically.

Such an approach not only contradicts Kierkegaard's self-conception. It also collides with the currently prevalent way of dealing with him. At a time when there is a widespread tendency to level the difference of philosophy and literature, argumentation and rhetoric, an author such as Kierkegaard, who was inseparably thinker and poet, must attract a new interest. What is primarily interesting today are precisely the forms of communication from which the following studies derive. I do not want to go beyond that. Interest in the forms of communication can claim to be the focus, because it was essential to the Dane himself. In England, where George Pattison is working,[2] a more satisfactory work on Kierkegaard than the substantively oriented reception after World Wars I and II may be imminent. But that tendency may also result from detaching forms from contents and withdrawing attention from the latter. The resulting detachment cheats Kierkegaard out of his best quality, his seriousness. Impressed by this seriousness, the subject of my dissertation at the age of twenty-two,[3] I feel challenged to correct the inadequacy of the literature, even at the price of academic awkwardness. Thus, with conscious partiality, I am concerned with contents.

The inadequacy of Kierkegaard's self-conception should not be lost in the process. In terms of substance, it is inherent in the philosophical grasp of my studies. It may indeed be assumed that Kierkegaard would have been willing to concede that philosophy is contained in his Christian psychology of despair. But he undoubtedly relates the philosophical part of his work to the element subordinated in a whole, which is of a religious nature and colors even its aesthetic elements with religion. In contrast, I deal with his analysis of despair as a piece of philosophy which can be taken out of the whole to a certain extent. To rebut the objection that I thus alienate this analysis itself, the reference to my effort not to lose sight completely of its theological goal would certainly not help me very much. For theology, like philosophy, degrades Kierkegaard to a handmaiden. My procedure can be justified only by its intention to impart knowledge. In this book, I am concerned primarily not with Kierkegaard but with the issue. Hence, I make no moves to accomplish the fascinating task of searching for the traces of Kierkegaard's own despair, in the face of which he said that *The Sickness unto Death* directed him, as evidenced by his other writing.[4] I take him seriously by putting his contribution to the issue to a critical test. To a considerable extent, the criterion of the test is an alternative understanding of the issue.

On another point, my approach hopefully coincides with Kierkegaard's intention. When I told a clergyman relative of my plan, he asked me whether I also show how one gets out of despair. I had to disappoint him. My abrupt no, however, was only to stave off the expectation that, after the diagnosis, I would present suggestions for therapy, and I thought I had to reject such suggestions not least out of loyalty to Kierkegaard. No doubt, Kierkegaard does talk of the person in despair as a physician talks of his patient, and the rhetorical extravagance of his book itself serves to redeem his claim in the Preface to assimilate "everything Christian" in his representation to "a physician's lecture at a sick-bed." But he does not let any advice for recovery follow from his address to the patient. He does indeed mean to be able to refrain from that because, in his anatomy of despair itself, he has already shown what promises a cure. Anti-Climacus, the alleged author of the book, "only describes the illness, by constantly defining what 'faith' is."[5] According to Kierkegaard, this faith and only this faith would guarantee health. Yet the fact that Anti-Climacus treats it not on its own but only in and with the gradual production of the idea of despair also means that he describes it and does not stipulate it. According to his claim, at any rate, from the start he operates descriptively and does not relate prescriptively to the reader at the end, either. In the description of his procedure, Kierkegaard refers to belief to indicate that he rebukes the person in despair not out of a theologically dogmatic borrowing, but rather out of what the theologians call "faith," manifest in the movements of existence blocked in despair. If one wants to experience how one gets out of his despair, one need not consult any doctrine of faith; one need only *make* these movements. Kierkegaard describes them so exactly that they can be made even by someone who does not even know that the theologians connect the idea of faith with them.

This book comprises previously unpublished material. The first study was a lecture I delivered in June 1992 at a Kierkegaard conference at the Institute for Ethics and Philosophy of Religion of the University of Aarhus. In October 1992, it was discussed in a seminar in Oslo.[6] It was originally intended for an (as yet) unrealized collection. The second study and the conclusion were written right after the first. Even though—for reasons mentioned above—the book is divided into three parts that form relatively contained units, the book has been designed as a whole. The first published English treatment of Kierkegaard's negativistic method is also part of the whole.[7] It exposes the methodical structure of *The Sickness unto Death* and, mainly from its beginning with the self, gives an interpretation I do not spell out here again. But after it had appeared in German as a monograph,[8] I wanted to spare the pressured publisher a republication. Its connection with this book can be explained by its title. Even when it appeared, I had a book about despair in mind. That is why I avoided presenting it as a study of despair. It was to be incorporated into the book as an introduction explaining the methodological and anthropological assumptions of Kierkegaard's analysis of despair, without discussion of them per se. Only when the German publisher insisted on the word "despair" did I add the subtitle: *Das Selbst auf dem Grund der Verzweiflung* [*The Self on the Basis of Despair*]. This expresses the fact that the immediate subject is not despair, but rather the self. On the other hand, the subject of this book can be formulated thus: *Despair on the Basis of the Self*. The studies seek despair on a basis that is at the same time removed from the self.

In this book, the treatment of Kierkegaard's negativistic method could have been included only in a revision. This is not because I see many things differently today and would depict them differently. Essentially, I think I can maintain my thesis. Instead, a revision would be necessary because of the uniformity of the way of thinking. That treatment refers to the text; these studies, on the other hand, move as it were at a moderate distance to the text. Their strategy is not based solely on the conviction that only such alternatives are visible to the proposed position. They are produced mainly from the hope that only by withdrawing from direct claims can the issue, even Kierkegaard's issue, be seen as clearly as I think it deserves.

I am grateful to the students in my 1992 summer semester on *The Sickness unto Death*. Their interest impelled me to interrupt a bigger work and present my "Corrections of Kierkegaard" for discussion again. Thanks to Kathrin Hönig and Christoph Kurth for their help. Special thanks to Friedhelm Herborth for accepting the little book into the publication schedule on short notice.

Berlin, November 1992
M.T.

First Study

The Existential Dialectical Basic Assumption of Kierkegaard's Analysis of Despair

I

1. In recent decades, our understanding of the philosophy of philosophers such as Kant or Hegel has been enriched by various attempts at a reconstruction that reveals the argumentative structure of fundamental texts and presents the ideas expressed in them more comprehensibly. Thus far, the philosophical interpretation of Kierkegaard has not exhibited any comparable attempts. The following considerations cannot fill the gaps, either. However, they might stimulate more productive engagement with Kierkegaard. I would like to reconstruct the representation of despair given by *The Sickness unto Death* (1849)[1] so that it can be grasped from a single premise.[2] The reconstruction is aimed primarily at exposing Kierkegaard's hidden intentions and facilitating a rational debate with his analysis of despair through a cautious correction of his conceptualization. Such a reconstruction may also demonstrate the line of argumentation of his analysis more clearly. Yet my essay can only be a first step on the path to the required translation into clearer concepts. Here, I have to make do with formulating the assumptions themselves in referring to—but also distanced from—the text, and I have to do without a conceptual restruc-

turing of the edifice supported by it. The self-restraint in fulfilling the task of transformation necessarily results from an economical circumscription of the material. In the framework of the first study, not much more than the introductory proposition to the analysis can be reformulated.[3] The more advanced stages of the analysis are to be considered only insofar as Kierkegaard elucidates the fundamental principle [*Grundsatz*] in them. The concrete forms, whose description concludes his philosophy of despair, can be discerned from the start only in outline. The external scaffolding on which Kierkegaard hangs concrete terms by subsuming them under the initial schema is apparent, but the internal arrangement of the scaffolded edifice is not.[4]

The lack of awareness for the premise to be exposed is to be blamed for the lack of a fully or even historically convincing discussion of Kierkegaard's analysis of despair. In the philosophical interpretation of Kierkegaard, the prevailing tendency is to constrict the history of origin of this drastically underestimated thinker to his dependence on German idealism, and consequently to regard the history of his effect from a truncating perspective. From that premise, a perspective is opened onto a larger context of tradition. It is at least to be sketched at the end in a typological simplification. Moreover, it is to be indicated how and where Kierkegaard's approach entered into the later philosophy of existence. For a redefinition of the historical place of his treatise on despair, the comments about the history of his origin and effect perform a preliminary work at best. They would have to be expanded and deepened in various directions. Thus, in light of the interpretation offered here, it seems virtually imperative to compare the thesis of *The Sickness unto Death* with Schopenhauer's statement that we humans first say yes to life, to which we should say no. In terms of content, the relationship to Schopenhauer deserves even more attention than all references to Fichte, Schelling, and Hegel, important as these may be in a formal respect. But alongside the reconstruction placed in the center, and the localization pushed to the margins, are two further areas of study, which must remain completely untreated for the time being. Before we enter into the territory to be conquered, I should nonetheless delineate them for a comprehensive orientation.

One of the two fields we cannot enter here is, as it were, at the back of the area that can be developed. The attempt to derive Kierkegaard's analysis of despair from a single premise does not go behind this. The reconstruction stops where the premise itself would have to be questioned about its truth-content. It is left to another kind of reflection to test whether the premise holds up at all, and if it does hold up, how what is stated as fact in it is justified. The other of those two fields is not as directly related to the subject of this first study. We would get to it only in the process of transcending the basis of reconstruction. This is the field of an ultimate transcending critique. The reconstruction will also have to be critical. But an immanent critique flows merely into it, one that—more than correcting a conceptual framework not always appropriate to its own intentions—insists on asking what it is that Kierkegaard is committed to by his own premise. A transcending critique would, on the other hand, have to start by exposing all the premises hidden in the text, not only those that are basic for the reconstruction, and then to discover to what extent the analysis burdened with all these premises does justice to its subject matter. It is transcending especially in exceeding the phenomenon usually designated as despair. As a result of abstaining from it, the reconstruction remains within the boundaries of its designated approach.

2. According to the title, Kierkegaard's final analysis of despair is to be reconstructed from its existential-dialectical fundamental premise. Before I say what I think the analysis presupposes, I should mention briefly what *type* of premises I have in mind. Kierkegaard makes many assumptions in his 1849 book. His

theological preliminary decisions form one kind of assumptions, another is the three anthropological premises he introduces right at the start: that man is first a synthesis, second has a self, and third, one that is established by God.[5] Even though the two types of premises are the most apparent ones, they are not my immediate subject matter. I already presuppose them. That means in the case of the theological preliminary decisions: I accept as a fact that the premise I select as a central theme is itself motivated by theological preliminary decisions.[6] And for the anthropological premises, that means that I assume that the three initial theses, as I have tried to show on a previous occasion,[7] are simply *hypo*theses, which formulate the necessary conditions man must fulfill to be able to despair, and that consequently, they find their later justification only later in the analysis of despair.

The premises with which Kierkegaard approaches the phenomenon itself shall be examined against the background of the theological preliminary decisions and the anthropological premises. The premises of this third type basically coincide with Kierkegaard's prejudgments about how we relate factically to the two dimensions of our being referred to by the anthropological premises, that is, to our being human and our established self. They fall into the sphere which Heidegger would contrast as the existentiell-ontical one of consummating Dasein against the existential-ontological sphere of the constitution of Being of Dasein. Contrary to Heidegger's view, Kierkegaard considers human Dasein both in an existentiell and existential way: his view is existential in the preliminary projection of those dimensions of Being, and existentiell in the analysis of our relation to them. The difference between the existential and existentiell perspective can be seen most clearly in the self, which for itself is nothing but a relating itself-to-itself.[8] The person must also relate to the fact that he is determined purely as the relation's relating itself-to-itself, and this secondary relation is the existentiell one, into whose framework Kierkegaard inserts despair. The search for a *fundamental* premise is informed by the supposition that all axioms of the third type can ultimately be traced back to a single one. I call this fundamental premise existential-dialectic not only because Kierkegaard designates his whole concern a dialectic of existence,[9] but also because and primarily with regard to the dialectic of an existence that has a refracted relation to its own structure.[10] The existential-dialectical principle of Kierkegaard's analysis of despair is: *We do not will to be directly what we are.* The principle clearly requires elucidation: (a) What does it mean to say *we* do not want to be what we are? About whom is Kierkegaard speaking?[11] (b) What does it mean to say that we do not will to be what we *are*? What kind of being is that to which we allegedly relate negatively? (c) How is it to be understood that we do not will to be *what* we are? And finally: (d) In what sense do we will all this *not to be*?

(a) According to Kierkegaard's self-conception, the question about the subject of the proposition could be answered adequately only by recourse to his theological preliminary decisions. That is, the only adequate answer for him can only be: we who live in the state of sin. But the inadequate answer we can give by disregarding Kierkegaard's theology of sin is not to be found in *The Sickness unto Death*, either. Only with the help of other texts can the subject of the proposition be supplemented somewhat historically: we who live in that Europe at the end of modernity which only imagines itself to be Christian. Nonetheless, the supplementation does not merely come from outside. In his 1849 treatise, Kierkegaard does not deal with the historical situatedness of the subject because he also presupposes it, and he does that for the same reason that he presupposes sinfulness.[12] He does both by restricting himself consistently to that point in the system granted to his treatise in the introduction to *The Concept of Anxiety*. In the secret systematic of Kierkegaard's works,

The Sickness unto Death assumes the position of a second ethics, whose classification in the whole follows the model of Schelling's second positive philosophy.[13] Consequently, together with the dogmatics, of which Kierkegaard says this explicitly, *The Sickness unto Death* presupposes the whole facticity, which already for Schelling was a historical one and which goes as far back as the primeval fact of the loss of original nature.

The other questions about the fundamental principle can be clarified by means of the existential definitions of our text. However, even the methodological abstraction from Kierkegaard's theological preliminary decisions compels us toward the preliminary epoch of the definition of being established by God.[14] On the other hand, it seems to make sense to differentiate Being over against the self and to place in it—beyond our being human—our pre-given Dasein. Kierkegaard never abandoned his originally dichotomous approach in his conception of self-becoming as a consummation of the pre-given Dasein in reality, but rather integrated it into the trichotomous schema, according to which the self overarches the two opposing elements of the synthesis.

(b) The being, to which we allegedly relate negatively, thus contains three aspects: we do not will to be what we are as a self, what we are in our being human, and what we are in our pre-given Dasein. Our Dasein is to be understood in a very broad sense. It is not only the Dasein *as what* we find ourselves, but rather also includes that *in which* we find ourselves.[15] Characterized in this way, it is a Dasein that is in any case determined by the past. But the Dasein as what we find ourselves also has a bearing on the future, insofar as all our dispositions and potentialities belong to it, and the Dasein in which we find ourselves pertains to the whole present world. Here, even the presupposed history projects *into* the field of inquiry of *The*

THE EXISTENTIAL BASIC ASSUMPTION   7

Sickness unto Death. The Dasein *as what* we find ourselves is suffused with the traces of our life history, and the Dasein *in which* we find ourselves opens as a world toward its history, toward world history.

(c) Not least in view of its historical concretion is it to be taken seriously that Kierkegaard imputes to us a negative relation to *what* we are. The Being to which we allegedly relate negatively is hardly restricted to facticity, to pure Dasein. Along with Hegel, Kierkegaard at least explicates Dasein in terms of a determinateness which as such is a what-determinateness. Insofar as we do not will to be what we are in our pre-given Dasein, we relate negatively to our individual determinateness. Analogously, it could be said: insofar as we do not will to be what we are in our being human, we relate negatively to our particular determinateness, to what usually inheres in the specific difference of the human species vis-à-vis all entities, that is, to having a synthetically composed Being. Only on the level of the self does Being mean facticity. However, first this facticity is the special facticity of the self—that is, that we always already have to relate to ourselves—and second Kierkegaard considers facticity in terms of determinateness as *in*determinateness.[16] The self we directly do not will to be is the abstract or negative self, whose negativity is based on its indeterminateness.[17] Kierkegaard commits the error of expanding this concept of self in the direction of a concrete self which in truth merely designates the Dasein that is without a place in the outline of the system.[18] We need to correct his error because only the indeterminateness of the self explains the not-willing-to-be genuinely directed at it. It explains it from the fear of nothingness, which Kierkegaard tacitly takes from his first anthropological text over into the second.

(d) This not-willing-to-be reflects in itself the difference of determinateness and indeterminateness. We do not want to be—that implies in relation to our pre-given Dasein and being human that we want not to assume and accept it. On the other hand, in relation to our self it implies that we want to get rid of it. As a result of that error, Kierkegaard makes the next one of expanding the concept of willing-to-get-rid-of-oneself to the not-assuming-and-accepting the pre-given Dasein. This error is also to be corrected. For, first, to refuse to assume and accept is temporally distinct from willing to get rid of oneself. The will to get rid of oneself is, as it were, at the end. We want to put an end to freedom, as Kierkegaard defines the self; we do not want to continue the process we are entangled in, insofar as each of us is always already installed in his self-establishing. On the other hand, not to will to accept oneself is at the beginning. We do not even want to begin to be the individuals and humans that we are. Second, to refuse to assume and accept is also distinct from willing to get rid of ourselves in terms of motive. It is motivated not by a fear of indeterminateness, but rather by a revulsion against the limitations of determinateness. In appropriating Hegel's insight into the determinateness of Dasein, Kierkegaard also changes it by identifying it with limitation. We do not want to accept our Dasein and being human because we revolt against the limitations thus set.

II

With this elucidation of the fundamental principle, the real tasks set for us by this principle are indicated at best. I can tackle here only the two I referred to at the beginning, the reconstruction of Kierkegaard's analysis of despair and the determination of its historical place. This is a reconstruction—which now means more closely reconstruction of the theory—as the analysis of despair of *The Sickness unto Death* may be regarded—from its fundamental premise that we moderns do not want to be what we are in the sense elucidated. What the reconstruction is entrusted with entered even into the elucidation of the axiom itself: to expose hidden intentions and to introduce clearer concepts. But the reconstruction of that theory no longer has to do that in dealing with the principle to be presupposed, but rather with all the propositions that result from the premise. Two things are basically to be expected from it. On the one hand, from its *con*structive side, it is to demonstrate that essential parts of the theory gain persuasive power if they are read as consequences of the fundamental premise. On the other hand, from its *de*structive side, it is to prove that, to be able to persuade, parts of the theory must be reformulated according to the criteria of the fundamental premise.

The reconstruction of the theory of despair outlined in *The Sickness unto Death* can be oriented toward the proposed compartmentalization of Being, to which we relate negatively, into the pre-given Dasein, the being human, and the self. After going through these three dimensions of being in despair interpreted in terms of an existential dialectic, I will, in a fourth point, see whether it holds up by moving Kierkegaard's conception of *not*-being-in-despair into the perspective of his fundamental principle.

1. The bulk of the material to be organized is precisely in the conceptually unaccentuated dimension of our relationship to our pre-given Dasein. Kierkegaard's theory stands or falls on a twofold distinction, on the differentiation of an authentic and an inauthentic despair, and especially the internal structuring of authentic despair in the two forms of a despaired willing to be oneself and an equally despaired not willing to be oneself. But the uncapitalized little word "self" means whatever I am in my pre-given Dasein.[19] Since it is found on almost every page of *The Sickness unto Death*, almost every page talks of the despaired relation to the pre-given Dasein. Indeed, it includes a good deal

more than that. For Kierkegaard often chooses the term "the Self" or "a Self," where the uncapitalized "self" would be appropriate.[20] In a way, his inflationary use of the concept of self reproduces the error he commits by expanding the abstract to a concrete self. For the so-called concrete Self is nothing but the pre-given Dasein. It is just that the inflation exacerbates matters insofar as it blurs the boundary separating the scope of the existential-ontological determinations from the existentiell-ontical sphere. For it is by no means the case that the "Self" rightly understood merely nominalizes the fact that the uncapitalized "self" designates. It concerns several facts. If the substantive is a cipher for the pure process of relating oneself to oneself, then the pronoun used as an apposition refers to that *to which* a person relates if he relates to his pre-given Dasein.

1.1 After this pre-clarification, let us turn first to the two forms of authentic despair. If there is something to what was said, not to will to be oneself can only mean: we do not will to be what we are in our pre-given Dasein. That would guarantee that what is presupposed in the accepted principle is in fact a subject mater of the theory. But is it also that which is fundamentally presupposed and which fundamentally comprises everything else? At first sight, it appears as if not to will to be what we are is not even on the level of authentic despair the whole, but merely a part, limited by its opposite. Yet the appearance quickly dissolves. For the opposite cannot even be what it should be by the letter. To will to be what one is would have nothing despairing in it. Not directly in any case. At a very mediated stage, Kierkegaard does in fact analyze a despaired willing to be oneself that is worthy of the name.[21] But the willing to be a self that is, as it were, in despair all the same only develops out of the despairing willing to be a self unworthy of its name. This implies in truth: we will to be *what we are not*. The translation does not need to hide behind the author's back at all. Kierkegaard himself translates the immediately despaired willing to be a self into a willing to be of what we are not.[22]

What we will to be here is, in his language, a constructed or hypothetical self, that is, an existence that by arbitrary selection is only partially determined or stripped completely of its determinateness, one that has little or nothing to do with our factical existence.[23] The willfully expropriated existence can be degraded secondarily by surrendering oneself to the determinateness of another individual or can be exalted by its self-sacrifice for the indeterminateness of an abstraction.[24] Then it becomes clear that in despairingly willing to be a self, we simply want to be what we are not. We want to be it in a perverted form of accepting, in an appropriation not of what is our own but of what is of the other.

Naturally, the question arises as to why Kierkegaard introduces a willing to be a self that he has to translate and yet introduces it an untranslated form. One answer is given by his assertion that in despair to will to be a self would be impossible without the establishment of the self by God.[25] Just as Kierkegaard's "No" to any system is ambivalent, so is his rejection of philosophical proofs of the existence of God half-hearted. Secretly, he would like to prove the existence of God by way of the existence of despair.[26] That is, one proof for the divine power that established the self is to be provided by the despaired willing to be a self. But as a willing to be what we are not, in despair to will to be a self does not provide this proof. Just as Kierkegaard provides allegedly reasonable thoughts, which in truth rest on theological presuppositions, so, in turn, we also find arguments that he justifies theologically even though they are not evident in themselves. One of these, in terms of its primary content, is the dictum of a despairing willing to be a self. We can be in despair such that we do not want to be what we are, without relating ourselves consciously or unconsciously to a God. Our negative self-relation becomes a negative relation to God only if this kind of despair assumes the quality of a willing to be oneself worthy of the name. For then it turns into a revolt against the Creator of our individually determined Dasein. At the same moment, however, it leaves behind everything it initially was. Instead of transforming our pre-given Dasein, we now *insist on* it, but only to disavow our Creator.[27]

Now, Kierkegaard broaches the initial willing to be what we are not under the rubric of a despaired willing to be a self, because he projects the revolt against the Creator back onto it. Clearly, this is served by the later translation of the despairing willing to be oneself into a despair of defiance together with the simultaneous renaming of the despairing not willing to be oneself into a despair of weakness.[28] At first glance, the translation seems to be without problems. No doubt, a certain defiance is also blended in the willing to be what we are not. But this defiance is different from the defiance of rebellious despair. Kierkegaard hints at the difference by saying of this despair that here we want to be ourselves not simply *in* defiance, but rather *for* spite.[29] Yet he does not seem willing to absolve the wanting to be what we are not from a negative relation to God. The reason for that most likely is that through that distinction he simply wants to distinguish a latent revolt against God from the manifest one. In truth, to will to be what we are not is not even characterized by a defiant revolt against God.[30] We have to return to the differences in the concept of defiance.

According to *The Sickness unto Death*, the two forms of authentic despair can be reduced to one another.[31] To a certain extent, the proposed reformulation puts us in a position to reconstruct their reciprocal reducibility. If we understand the despaired wanting to be self as a wanting to be what we are not, it is revealed as based motivationally in its opposite. We want to be what we are not because we do not want to be what we are. Otherwise, we would have no reason to substitute an imaginary Dasein for our factual one. Seen this way, not to will to be oneself provides the basis for, in despair, to will to be oneself. In a certain sense, the reverse is also true: we do not will to be what we are because we will to be what we are not. Otherwise there appears to be no reason to flee our factical existence. Seen this way, the so-called willing to be oneself takes priority over not willing to be oneself. Nevertheless, in the relation of the two forms, a curious asymmetry is maintained. That we will to be what we are not because we do not want to be what we are is always the case. On the other hand, it is by no means always and necessarily the case that we do not will to be what we are because we will to be what we are not. We can suffer under our existence without transforming it through another one. Thus, while in despair to will to be oneself is inconceivable without its opposite, in despair not to will to be oneself can occur independently of its other. It constitutes the original form of despair.

However, Kierkegaard not only refuses to allow primacy to in despair not to will to be oneself. He even privileges the other form, in despair to will to be oneself. That he first reduces not willing to be oneself to willing to be oneself and carries out the complementary reduction only in retrospect seems to betray his priorities in the issue. Apparently, he considers the despair of defiance as more original. Yet its privileging rests on a self-misunderstanding of the theory. Kierkegaard erroneously passes off as a characteristic feature of despairingly willing to be oneself what in reality characterizes *both* forms of authentic despair. He can be mistaken about this only because, as I have already suggested, he works with an ambiguous concept of defiance.

There are at least three kinds of defiance that have to be distinguished in *The Sickness unto Death*.[32] The rebellious defiance of in despair willing to be oneself, which is legitimately so called but is discussed only at the end, is preceded by that defiance attached to the willing to be oneself which is illegitimately so called, the position of one who in despair wills to be what he is not. That defiance consists in the arrogance of constructing one's own Dasein. To be able to prove the priority of the initial willing to be oneself, Kierkegaard would have to start with this defiance and demonstrate that there is a constructivist arrogance even in the so-called despair of weakness. Instead, by privileging in despair willing to be oneself, he orients himself to a third kind of defiance, the defiance of willing the impossible. But the defiance expressed in this, namely that we will what we cannot do and that we will it despite being conscious of our inability to do so, characterizes both forms of authentic despair and is not an exclusive feature of the allegedly prior form. For it is impossible not only to be what one is not; it is also impossible not to be what one is.[33] The impossible on the level of the pre-given Dasein and of being human is also ambivalently determined. On the level of the self it is also part of both forms. It is impossible to get rid of one's self.[34] But one wants to get rid of one's self both in despairingly willing to be oneself and in not willing to be oneself. Consequently, Kierkegaard does not privilege in despair to will to be oneself. He distinguishes only a certain kind of defiance. He demonstrates that the defiance of willing the impossible is more universal and thus also more fundamental than the defiance of the arrogant self-transformation and of the revolt against God.

Thus nothing has changed: inasmuch as the so-called despaired willing to be oneself is a willing to be what we are not, it is based, according to the hypothesis about the existential-dialectical basic premise, on not willing to be what we are. That we do not want to be what we are occupies the whole space of authentic despair.

1.2 Nevertheless, the full extent of the impotent capitulation to one's own existence does not seem to define the full extent of Kierkegaard's concept of despair. After all, aside from authentic despair, there is to be an inauthentic despair. But is there really? In the framework of a reconstruction, the question can be settled only within the boundaries of an examination of the internal consistency of the Kierkegaardian concept. Now, the concept of inauthentic despair presented in *The Sickness unto Death* is at least ambivalent. What is unequivocal is only that, by inauthentic despair, Kierkegaard means an unconscious despair. However, by unconscious despair he understands one in which a person is not conscious of *himself*, as well as one in which he is not conscious of his *despair*.³⁵ To be precise, he even puts a threefold unconsciousness into unconscious despair. For, on the side of that despair which is not accompanied by any consciousness of *it*, he differentiates between a lack of consciousness of *what* despair is and an unconsciousness *that* one's own state is despair.³⁶ But in the latter sense, there is no unconscious despair.³⁷ We can have an inadequate idea of despair; however, we cannot be in despair without somehow knowing it.³⁸

As a result, there is a serious issue addressed by the question of how the despair presupposed in the fundamental premise relating to inauthentic despair is the one that is not accompanied by any consciousness of *itself*. Naturally, here, too, it is to be ascertained how an unconscious despair is even possible. There cannot be despair without self-consciousness in the sense of an accompanying self-presence. A person in despair always has himself before him. The only conceivable despair is one whose subject is not conscious of himself insofar as he possesses no consciousness of self in the genuine Kierkegaardian meaning of the word, therefore no idea of what it means to be established, always already, in relation of oneself to oneself.³⁹ It is in this way that Kierkegaard introduces the concept of inauthentic despair.⁴⁰ After his initial definition, the concept is therefore not situated on the level of pre-given existence passed through here. If it is to be located on this level, it must be translated into the language of willing in which the concept of authentic despair is formulated.

Then, what is meant by it is likewise revealed as a not willing to be what we are but as a not willing of another kind. As persons in inauthentic despair, we will not to be ourselves insofar as we do not even begin establishing ourselves into a relation with our pre-given Dasein despair in which we are able to will or not will it. The not willing, which, as a form of authentic despair, constitutes the alternative to the willing that is not in despair, is itself basically a willing, that is, a willing in the mode of negation, of rejecting our pre-given existence. By contrast, the not-willing characteristic of inauthentic despair is not in any sense a willing; it simply does not achieve willing. It is true that the difference between one and the other kind of not willing forbids us simply to extend the fact that has proved basic in the analysis of authentic despair to the realm of inauthentic despair. But it also shows that in inauthentic despair not to will to be oneself has even less to do with rebellious defiance than does in authentic despair not to will to be oneself. Even though it is free of the arrogance of transformation, Kierkegaard can say that in authentic despair not to will to be oneself is characterized not only by the defiance of willing the impossible but also by rebellious defiance, because he also projects rebellion back onto the rejection. For that, the inauthentic despair affords no handle. For where no act of will occurs, there is no place for revolt, either. However, under inauthentic despair, even according to the criteria of the reconstructed theory, hardly more than a very weak despair may be imagined, the one with the lowest degree of intensity.[41] In the undifferentiated not willing we are in despair simply because of a dulled notion of the contradiction in which we find ourselves if we do not even establish ourselves into a relation of positively or negatively willing our existence.

2. According to the hypothesis, Kierkegaard assumes all the considerations used here in his analysis of despair: we, who refuse the assumption of our given Dasein, do not want to be what we are in our being human and as a self, either. As soon as Kierkegaard moves what we are into the perspective of our being human, he sees something fundamentally new in the basic facts of the case. He does this in the first course through the forms of despair, where he tries to explain the phenomenon from a failure of the synthesis constituting being human. What is new in the theoretical consideration of the synthesis becomes clearer in the second course through the forms of despair, which reformulates the phenomenon in terms of the theory of

consciousness, largely remaining close to the previously elucidated approach, more precisely, taking only a single step beyond the separation of an inauthentic despair from an authentic one, and beyond their internal differentiation in both forms, with which we are essentially concerned. In order for the innovative content of the first course to emerge cleary, this second course is sketched first at least briefly.

With its last step, the second course through the forms of despair goes beyond the approach expounded thus far insofar as it leads to the already envisaged point where someone wants to be oneself in a way that is really in despair, that is, in defiance of his Creator.[42] However, already with his first step in his theoretical consideration of consciousness does Kierkegaard dissolve the various forms differentiated at the beginning of his treatise into stages of a process. We can call the consideration aimed at the elements of the synthesis a structural-theoretical one, and a stage-theoretical one the one aimed at consciousness. Kierkegaard turns despair into a process by taking consciousness [*Bewusstsein*] for a level of awareness [*Bewusstheit*], which rises to the highest degree in the process of unfurling. The despair of one who wills to be himself in defiance of his Creator is coupled with the most extreme awareness. The main line of a process of becoming aware ending in a defiant revolt against God is interrupted, however, by deliberations in which Kierkegaard pauses, as it were, to pick up and modify a previously added distinction: that between a despair over something and a despair over oneself.[43] With the modifying exposition of this distinction, he in fact makes a new approach. But we can disregard it in the present context. The new approach is, as it were, developed inside a figure, which here shall be used only to display a background against which the first course of the argument shall unfold; hence we need only follow its external outlines. From such an external perspective, we may ascertain that at least the rough subdivision of the section is congruent with the familiar tripartite division: the processing despair begins as the latent one lurking in the lack of consciousness of one's own self, then becomes manifest as in despair not to will to be oneself, and climaxes in a despaired willing to be oneself.[44] Insofar as the second course through the forms of despair is thus connected with the beginning in the three basic forms, it is actually the first in the logic of the construction of the theory.

The identity obtaining at least externally or in conformity with the system of the three initially distinguished forms with the forms condensed into stages of a process shows that those three forms actually were already successive stages following one another. In this respect, too, Kierkegaard conceives the forms differently as understood in terms of a structural theory. Admittedly, the forms of despair emerging from a failure to accomplish the synthesis cannot appear simultaneously, either. No one who is in such despair that he lacks both necessity and finitude can simultaneously live through the conflicting despair that consists of lacking possibility and infinitude. But in the first course of his argument, Kierkegaard does not pursue a process. Whether a process takes place all the same in covertness is a question that must remain open for the time being. If it were to take place, it would in any case also be covert, and mainly one that was unintended. Kierkegaard not only avoids setting in motion what he sees as purely structural forms. He does not even begin to undertake an attempt to relate them at all to the forms set in motion. Thus, it is even more remarkable that the structural theory nonetheless does comprehend the forms of authentic despair just as they were reconstructed here: as not to will to be what we are, and as to will to be what we are not. Only it describes the reconstructed forms not with regard to a sequence in the process of existing, but rather in the perspective of a hierarchy in the logical-ontological construction of existence. In terms of a structural theory, to be in despair in all of its forms means both that we do not want to be what we are and that we want to be what we are not. We do not want to be what we are as human beings who are defined by both necessity and finitude as well as possibility and infinitude, and we want to be what we are not, that is, a pure possibility and infinitude, which in its purity is inhuman, or a pure necessity and finitude, which alienates us from our being human.

That the negative element in the loss of facticity or transcendence is based on a not willing to be what we are should be easily understood. Its motive is clearly the fear of the effort of holding the extremes together.[45] By contrast, it may be less understandable that the ostensibly positive element in fixating on facticity or transcendence is based on a willing to be what we are not. After all, it appears as if we were fixated on one element of our human existence. However, the structural analysis of despair is based on the assumption that neither facticity nor transcendence remains in isolation what they are as an element of the synthesis. The necessity that is freely available because of its relation to possibility descends to the level of the determinateness of things, and the concrete possibility that is in conjunction with necessity turns into an inhumanly abstract possibility. Consequently, what is added to the effort of consummating our being human is the yearning for what is, as it were, an inhuman existence. This Being is inhuman not only as one of ideas, on the one hand, and one of things, on the other.[46] For Kierkegaard being human includes a personality essentially distinct from the individuality of the pre-given Dasein. Accordingly, we already long for an inhuman existence when we merge into an impersonal collective or want to be submerged in the other. It is such a depersonalization that Kierkegaard primarily has in mind.[47] But in principle, both reification and volatilization into the ideal can still fit into the scheme of his structural theory.[48]

In any case, the connection between the loss and the fixation on facticity or transcendence is to be thought of in such a way that fear produces the longing for an existence alien to one's own person. *Primarily* we do not want to be what we are as humans, and only *secondarily* do we want to be what we are not.

Consequently, not to will to be what we are, even according to the synthetical-theoretical consideration, is the basic fact. It is precisely the new element in this consideration that confirms that Kierkegaard starts from the fundamental principle attributed to him here.

3. Not to will to be what we are is the starting point both on the level of our being human and on that of our pre-given Dasein, because on both levels it means that we do not even begin to want to accept ourselves. The initial not willing to accept oneself is confronted, toward the end, by the willing to be rid of oneself. It is as willing to be rid of oneself that the not willing to be what we are appears on the level of the self. We have already said that. Now we need only develop what is inherent in the final position of willing to be rid of oneself. To will to be rid of oneself is the end in the sense that it is simultaneously the whole. It is what all despair ultimately amounts to. For we want to be rid of ourselves even when we want to be what we are not. Therefore, Kierkegaard can call despair to be rid of oneself the formula for all despair.[49] Thoroughly consistent, he explicates all despair in terms of not willing to be what we are. However, insofar as it comprises its opposite, this not willing to be what we are is more than the immediate not willing. If it is the whole in the way described, then it is the end only as a result of a mediation generated by the theory. The theory reaches its destination, as it were, in willing to be rid of oneself, in the sense that it traces both the immediate not willing to be oneself and the immediate willing to be oneself back to that. As its own end, it reveals the willing to be rid of oneself precisely through its projection onto the level of the self. The theory thus exposes it as a foundation as such only for itself but not for the one in despair.

Yet to will to be rid of oneself designates a *real* end of despair, too. Kierkegaard examines the real aspect of his final position where he infers from it the *heightened* formula for despair.

There, the starting point of his considerations is the fact that while we want to be rid of ourselves, we cannot. To will to be rid of oneself may hold as a formula for all despair also because, as not being able to be rid of oneself, it subsumes in itself that willing of the impossible whose despair is representative of all despair in Kierkegaard. Our despair is heightened as soon as we, in turn, despair over not being able to be rid of ourselves.[50] But the reflection of despair is an infinite process. In every new despair we also undertake a new attempt to be rid of ourselves, and the futility of this attempt must plunge us once again into despair. This heightening also prescribes a *law* of heightening to which the progress of the issue is subject.[51] Ruled by the law of its constant reflection, despair takes action quite differently from the preliminary draft of its process. It does not change into the rebellious despaired wanting-to-be-self, but rather burrows deeper into the not-wanting-to-be-self, discovered by the theory as its reason. Therefore, Kierkegaard would probably have discarded a more comprehensive account if the real end had been more completely present to him. He considers it only if despair can be nothing beyond wanting to be rid of the self. On the other hand, he hardly refers it back to the beginning. In reality, wanting to be rid of the self stands mainly at the end of the real process of despair insofar as it always already assumes despair in all the forms described by Kierkegaard. We want to be rid of ourselves as those who, from the very beginning, did not want to accept ourselves; and the despair over oneself, which Kierkegaard occasionally equates with the impotent attempt to get rid of oneself,[52] is a despair over the inability to accept what we are.

4. We sink into ever deeper despair only when no help comes from above. Freedom of despair requires help from above, that is, a divine intervention, because by ourselves, we do not summon up the will to being ourselves. Kierkegaard defines not being in despair precisely as willing to be oneself.[53] It is pre-

cisely for this reason that his speaking of in *despair* to will to be oneself must not be left unchanged. To the extent that it means more than to will to be what we are not, namely that we put our bungled existence on display so as to indict our creator, we are not even dealing with a conclusion from the being in despair previously discussed, but rather with a perversion of not being in despair. This is shown by its closer definition. In accordance with his negativistic method, which has the negative indicate the positive,[54] Kierkegaard does not put more into not being in despair than the negation of the negative, that is, of being in despair. Not being in despair, which for that reason he also expresses negatively, is the pure mirror image of being in despair. On the level of our pre-given existence and our being human, not to be in despair means to accept oneself, and in the depth dimension of our self, it means to ground oneself in the power that has established the self. If on the former level it overcomes the not willing to accept oneself, here analogously it overcomes the willing to get rid of oneself, which from the perspective of being established appears as the attempt to break free from that power. Because the self forms the foundation of the whole, to accept oneself acquires its authentic meaning only from the act of establishing oneself. It is from here that to accept oneself becomes a self-humiliation before God.[55] By contrast, the spite with which someone asserts his Dasein against God, as he in actual despair wills to be himself, turns this humility into its opposite.[56] His desperation presupposes at least an idea of what it is not to be in despair, while usually, according to *The Sickness unto Death*, the not-being-in-despair which really is what it should be inversely presupposes despair.

    The thesis that we would in truth be free of despair only if we have gone through it,[57] also points at Kierkegaard's fundamental principle. The assertion it implies, namely that initially we are all in despair, by no means makes its justification depend on the assumption of the omnipresence of a despair that is not conscious of itself. To support it, all that is needed is to prove the fundamental principle that we do not immediately want to be what we are. Yet producing a proof for this is difficult enough as it is, and at this point I, like Kierkegaard, cannot produce it, at least on the level of philosophical argumentation.

III

1. The lengthy business of a reconstruction is now essentially complete. What has not yet been tackled is the task of locating the reconstructed theory historically. Kierkegaard probably thought he did not have to prove the fundamental principle of his theory of despair argumentatively because he relied on the evidence of his own self-experience. But surely the experience he had of himself as a person in despair was hardly purely private. If it is true that, by those who do not want to be what they are, Kierkegaard meant the people in the allegedly Christian Europe of the end of the modern age, then he himself at any rate must have believed that an epochal experience found expression in his personal experience. The history of the effect of his work shows how much this is in fact the case. His influence especially on existential philosophy could hardly have been so great if his personal experience were not part of an epochal experience that spread only in the period after him and that in its full breadth became a sounding board for his word. And existential philosophy is only the theoretically most concise form of a modernity whose Kierkegaardianism is also demonstrated by Kafka.

Seen from this modernity, *The Sickness unto Death* appears as the beginning of an epoch—which, despite all postmodernity, is still continuing—in the European process of an understanding of men about themselves and their life. In it, three epochs stand out more or less clearly. If it were permitted to transfer the term of self-realization from the later ones to the earliest one, they could be reduced to the following common denominator: in the first epoch, self-realization is understood as realizing a definition of man, and indeed in the conviction that in principle we are willing to realize our definition. The second epoch conceives of self-realization as an unfolding of our own individuality, starting from the analogous assumption that everyone wants to be the individual he is of his own accord. The third epoch also sees self-realization as an individualization. But it makes the counter assumption that first and for the most part, no one has the serious will to really be the individual that he is. The realization of a definition of man demanded in the first part is, of course, an individual process, just as the unfolding of individuality in the second and the individualization are. Only the goal to be realized, the definition of man himself, is something super-individual. In the later epochs, in contrast, the individual process of self-realization no longer has any super-individual result.

To be sure, the epochs overlap. The first epoch coincides with that of metaphysics so that even after the so-called end of metaphysics the idea of a definition of man remains valid wherever there is covert metaphysical thinking. Just as the whole of metaphysics, whose end is usually considered the consequence of a loss of meaning, has itself already reacted to a loss of meaning, so has the idea of a definition of man. The Platonic *work of the soul*, ἔργον τῆς ψυχῆσ, or the Aristotelian work of man, ἔργον τοῦ ἀνθρώπου,[58] responds to the decline of absolute norms in the century of the Sophists. The answer is a retreat to an "Ought" allegedly anchored in human existence. In this respect, despite any difference of the respective epochs, the further development in the course of which Being became an ever more exclusive standard was already implicit in the beginning. This also holds in view of the fact that in Plato and Aristotle the ἔργον is, as it were, retained in the ἐνέργεια, the work in effecting. Only in the post-antiquity tradition, where the notion of a definition of man originated, were the individuals committed to a work transcending the consummation of their existence. It is in revolt against this that the Renaissance emerged, bringing the beginning of the second epoch. But even Marx, Kierkegaard's contemporary and a thoroughgoing metaphysician, still recognizes a work detached from the individual life process, that is, the realization of the human species. And Kierkegaard himself transcended such an idea only on the path toward *The Sickness unto Death*.

The concept of anxiety emphasizes the spirit and not the self because it still adheres to the idea that the individuals are destined for something super-individual. The book on despair, in contrast, departs from classical anthropology. This is only ostensibly contradicted by the fact that it also calls on the individual to realize his being human. For it encourages only accepting and assuming a pure structure, but by no means completing a work. However, it distances itself even more resolutely from Renaissance individualism, which here and there still dominates in the first version of the theory of despair in *Either/Or*. To be sure, Kierkegaard still thinks individualistically. But subsequent to the theology of sin outlined in 1844, he puts individuality in *The Sickness unto Death* under a negative sign. As a pre-given one, individuality, once a source of infinite wealth, becomes a pathetic limitation. After all, the ideal of a boundless unfolding of individuality then also gives way to the idea of humbling oneself under one's own limitations. Even Kierkegaard's willing to be oneself is in its humility the opposite of a will to power, that is, the broken willing of what is not willed, bearing in mind the impotence of willing the impossible.[59] Perhaps the genuine Christian motif of this alternative to Renaissance individualism has kept the author of *The Sickness unto Death* from abandoning completely the idea of a definition of man. At any rate, in his approach, classical anthropology continues to have an effect in the determinateness he interprets as limitation. It is still alive not in the question about being human as such but in the question about the determinateness both of being human and of individual existence. For it still maintains an interest in the "what"-content. It is chiefly because of its essentialism that *The Sickness unto Death* marks only the beginning of the epoch which found its most telling expression in existentialism.

2. Limiting myself to this paradigm, I would like to conclude by sketching with a few brief strokes the transformation of the Kierkegaardian approach in Heidegger's *Being and Time* and in Sartre's *Being and Nothingness*. The transformation of *The Sickness unto Death* seems instructive precisely because Heidegger and Sartre, unlike Jaspers,[60] do not exploit the treatise on despair as openly as they use the treatise on anxiety. In Heidegger's case, the anonymity of the reference to the treatise on despair is connected with his tendency to restrict the competence of the dialectician of existence to the existentiell-ontical realm. In fact, the way in which *Being and Time* reinterprets despair as an existentiell phenomenon can be seen only if we recognize first of all the way Heidegger seeks to absorb even Kierkegaard's existential-ontological project.[61]

2.1 On the existential-ontological level, Heidegger's link is the self. In *The Sickness unto Death*, the two elements constituting the self were the relation of oneself to oneself and the state of being established.[62] Heidegger explicates the relation of oneself to oneself in terms of existentiality, according to which Dasein in its Being is concerned with this very Being, and the fact of being established in terms of the concept of facticity according to which Dasein in each case has its being to be and has to be its Being as its own.[63] The ostensible redundancy in phrases such as those that Dasein in its Being is concerned with this very Being and that it has to be its own Being is important for Heidegger's case because it indicates his aspiration to eliminate the what-content retained by Kierkegaard and to commit Being, which after all has also discarded the name of man, to its pure being.[64] To be sure, the innovation is not exhausted in such a reduction. As for the fact of being established, Heidegger may make do with working out the pure facticity while disregarding the being-established through the completely other. He does this by reading the Being-toward in two ways: a "Having to be" and, less loud and almost coy, an "Ought-to-be," which retains from the old idea of a definition of man at least the doctrine that Dasein, as one that is delivered over to its own being,[65] also bears responsibility or has to correspond to a claim inherent in its being. But by translating the relating itself-to-itself into a "going around," Heidegger goes beyond mere explication. He discloses a willing-to-be more primordial than in despair to will to be oneself and not to will to be oneself, which, in *The Sickness unto Death*, was overformed by an idealistic model of reflection.[66] To be sure, Kierkegaard conceives the self itself as will. But it is only in *Being and Time* that this insight breaks through: even when we do not want to be ourselves, we still *want* to—in the sense that we are concerned with our being. Apparently, Heidegger also avoids saying that we are concerned with ourselves and that we have to be ourselves because he wants to distinguish the existentially fundamental willing to be from its existentiell modification.

Quite like Kierkegaard, on the existentiell level, Heidegger starts out from the not willing to be oneself. In his terms, that means: he starts with the inauthentic Dasein.[67] Even though despair does not occur in *Being and Time*, Kierkegaard's interpretation guides all the statements about inauthenticity made in it. This is shown most conspicuously by Heidegger's analysis of the movement from which the inauthentic Dasein results, the movement of falling prey to the world and the "they." Here, Heidegger orients himself to the remarks in *The Sickness unto Death* about the despair of necessity and finitude.[68] Not only are the features of his view of the world and the "they" shaped by Kierkegaard. Another Kierkegaardian aspect is that he combines falling prey to the world and falling prey to the "they" into a single movement and describes the inauthentic Dasein as one that falls prey to the world interpreted by the others.[69] Now, in all that, he repeats the existential-dialectical fundamental principle. Taken for itself, falling prey betrays this: we want to be what we are not. But the motif of falling refers back to the fact that we first do not want to be what we are. After all, it arises from Dasein's fleeing from itself.[70] That we do not want to be what we are and want to be what we are not Heidegger understands as stipulated for him by the context of that despair of necessity and finitude. It has its place in the course of the analysis oriented to the failure of the synthesis. Accordingly, Kierkegaard sees in it that we primarily do not want to be what we are in our being human, and therefore, secondarily, want to be what we are not. In tracing back the falling to Dasein's fleeing from itself, Heidegger copies this figure. But limiting himself to Kierkegaard's synthetic-theoretical perspective has the result that, in his view of inauthenticity, not willing to be oneself really does become the whole that encroaches on its other. There is no counterpart in *Being and Time* to the form of despair that Kierkegaard correctly describes as a despaired willing to be a self.

Moreover, Heidegger's construction of inauthenticity according to the model of the synthetic-theoretical view may be a reason why he banned despair as such from the circle of the ontologically relevant phenomena of Dasein. For even the model text seldom mentions real despair.[71] However, Heidegger seems to disregard it also because in a way he downgrades not willing to be oneself to the level of inauthentic despair, so that he leaves only its inauthenticity. The so-called universality of despair, established in *The Sickness unto Death* from the ubiquity of a despair allegedly not conscious of itself, is identified in *Being and Time* as being averageness;[72] and that we, as we said here, do not *directly* want to be what we are is captured by Heidegger in the stereotypical statement that Dasein falls prey to the openly interpreted world *first and mostly*: first, insofar as it is always already fallen; mostly, insofar as it usually also remains fallen.

But *The Sickness unto Death* contains not only sources from which Heidegger draws; it also provides a criterion for our judgment about Heidegger. The motif of fleeing from oneself marks at once the point at which we must decide between Kierkegaard and Heidegger.[73] Heidegger proceeds in rather a different way from not willing to be oneself than merely finding in it the first and principal thing in the reality to be represented. He also takes his starting point from not willing to be oneself insofar as he chooses it as a methodological guide for the description. In particular, he continues to describe the existential alternative to inauthenticity, the authentic Dasein, exclusively from the perspective of not willing to be oneself. What authentic Dasein consists of results solely from an analysis of the movement of fleeing. Heidegger wants to show it from that in the face of which we flee.[74] Thus, he commits himself to Kierkegaard's method, which traces the willing to be oneself that can never solidify into being oneself from being in despair and merely presents it as not being in despair. However, Heidegger does not fulfill his commitment. He deviates from Kierkegaard's own path by projecting authentic Dasein as being factically nonetheless independent of inauthentic Dasein. As a result, he gets entangled in an insoluble contradiction with his own approach. He exposes the contradiction himself. The attempt to derive authentic Dasein from that in the face of which is fled is linked with the pledge not to hold up to us humans any substantive ideal of existence and to force it on us from outside.[75] At the same time, in the actual elaboration of his doctrine of authentically being oneself, Heidegger does invoke precisely such an ideal.[76] But authenticity modeled on his ideal of existence is the opposite of that authenticity which would have come into focus if he had strictly complied with his methodological postulate. The alternative to the Dasein fleeing from itself can only be the Dasein accepting itself in Kierkegaard's sense. Yet here in *Being and Time* it is replaced by the heroic Dasein, which no longer shows any signs of the humiliation of accepting oneself.[77]

2.2 Sartre's early philosophy can be interpreted as an attempt to realize more consistently the negativism of fundamental ontology surrendered by Heidegger.[78] Sartre undertakes this attempt in a constant debate with Kierkegaard. His thesis that consciousness is not what it is and is what it is not strikes the note played in endless variations by his book of 1943; and insofar as this is the case, *Being and Nothingness* also plays a single coda to Kierkegaard's book of 1849. Sartre reads *The Sickness unto Death* on the basis of a four-fold correction to Heidegger's reception of Kierkegaard. First, he calls the willing not verbalized in *Being and Time* by name. Insofar as he also liberates the primal willing, in which Dasein is concerned with its own Being, from anonymity, the identification of the willing is already part of a more comprehensive strategy: immune to the temptation to shift the dialectic of existence onto the merely existentiell realm, Sartre secondly acknowledges the ontological relevance of Kierkegaardian figures of thought. Third, even where he puts these figures into an existentiell context, he confers on them a depth effect reminiscent of Kierkegaard, in the face of which the distinction between "existentiell" and "existential" loses its power. Fourth, in this area, he restores despair to new life.

To a *new* life—that is: in Sartre, despair assumes a form in which it looks quite different and yet corresponds structurally with its prototype. Its successor mainly is *bad faith* [*mauvaise foi*].[79] Bad faith is existentially primordial insofar as it initially discloses the dialectical structure of a consciousness that is not what it is, and is what it is not; and, like Kierkegaard's despair, it is at the same time an existentiell self-relation of a negative kind insofar as it abuses this structure. According to Sartre, one is untruthful in the sense of bad faith, either such that, while acknowledging not to be what one is, one does not will to be it in the mode of the "in-itself" [*En-Soi*]; or such that, while realizing to be what one is not, one yet also wills this being as a being-in-itself [*être-en-soi*]. Thus, bad faith is a self-*dis*guising, based on a distorted idea of one's own being, of the being-for-itself. It becomes a successor to Kierkegaard's despair because of the part that the willing plays in such a disguising idea. With it, Sartre wants to show that men can take up negative positions with respect to themselves.[80] But the determinate negativity of such positions resides in a negative willing, in that of self-denial. It is the will to deny one's own being directing that abuse that illuminates the proximity to Kierkegaard. After all, according to *The Sickness unto Death*, it is despair that realizes the relation to oneself as a misrelation.[81]

In a certain sense, Sartre even incorporates Kierkegaard's theological conception of sin. For in his theory of bad faith, the thought recurs that in the Fall of Man, the first use of freedom coincided with its abuse. And by that—just as Kierkegaard against his own intention does in the treatises on anxiety—Sartre also turns freedom into a necessity. Not only does he renew the opposition of despair and belief through his distinction of bad faith from *good faith* [*bonne foi*]. Secretly, he also bases the belief as *faith in* the more elementary belief of a *croyance*, which is itself a disturbed belief [*croyance troublée*], because in it, the belief to believe as consciousness is always already beyond itself.[82] What is tacitly behind this is the thesis: The being of consciousness is reflected in the consciousness of this being as a result of the necessary disturbance of such an ambiguous belief on its part with necessity as bad faith. That bad faith as an existential consummation of the structure of consciousness is itself formative of structure seems to be based in the ontological necessity with which freedom is abused in it.

Sartre naturally brings up the motif of a sinful despair only with the intention of extricating an attitude such as that of bad faith from the clutches of the theology of sin. The abuse of freedom is to be justified by an ontologization. In this respect, Sartre goes against the grain of *The Sickness unto Death*. This is shown in the movement of thought of his book. His reinterpretation of Kierkegaard constitutes a reversal of the course taken by *The Sickness unto Death*. At the beginning of this course was the insight that we do not will to be what we are, or even will to be what we are not; at the end, Kierkegaard called on us to will to be what we are, to accept ourselves in our finitude. If we interpret analogously the path pursued by Sartre in his first major work, that is, not as a chronology of his presentation but as the logic of his idea of the process that increasingly elucidates more of what we really want, then we may first state: however much it is modified, Sartre puts at the beginning the act which, in Kierkegaard's view, we are to reach at the end. For him, the initial act is the internal negation of things, through which consciousness is first of all constituted.[83] I become I by saying, as it were, to myself: I am not what I am not, and thus meaning: I *do not want to be* what I am not. That I do not want to be the things around me holds up on the basis of a philosophy that does not weaken Kierkegaard's destruction of the idea of a stable self-being, as fundamental ontology does, but rather strengthens it, as the only possible form in which I can be myself already at the beginning. The identity mediated by my non-identity with things—an implausible ideal of authenticity, if stated positively—defines, in Sartre, the self-hood that remains anonymous, through which the "for-itself" gains ground vis-à-vis the being-in-itself and to which it owes its name. But in Sartre's view, we ultimately want to be more than such a "for-itself." We want to be it in such a way as if it were *in*-itself, not simply the nothing of negation, but a being resting in itself. For Sartre, this means: ultimately, we want to be God.[84] Thus, he shifts to the end what for Kierkegaard was the beginning. In the end, we want to be what we are not, such that we do not want to be what we are: a for-itself incapable of justifying itself.

Like Kierkegaard's despairing willing, this willing wants something impossible in the consciousness of its impossibility. Therefore, it objectively constitutes despair in Kierkegaard's sense. However, Sartre does not just acquit the desire to become God of *sin*. By that, he also dismisses its desperation. Outside the horizon of the theology of sin, the fact that in the end we want the impossible per se really seems no longer a proof of our desperation, but rather evidence of a tragedy, which became unrecognizable when theology branded necessary guilt as sin. Sartre's sublation of despair into tragedy at once circumvents Kierkegaard's critique of it. Since in despair to will the impossible appears no longer as an ethically accountable transgression of oneself but as the completion of man's humanity, the diagnosis of his time that we do not want to be what we are is enveloped in the semblance of an eternal truth, before which all criticism must fall silent.

Second Study

On the Transcending Critique of Kierkegaard's Analysis of Despair

I

1. The study of the fundamental principle underlying the analysis of despair presented in *The Sickness unto Death* grounded the analysis on the theorem: we do not want to be what we are. Its main subject matter was the starting point of the analysis at which Kierkegaard stakes out the framework for his further considerations by separating inauthentic from authentic despair and especially by subdividing the latter into the two forms of a despaired not-willing to be oneself and an even more despaired willing to be oneself. The goal was to trace the whole as differentiated into the three forms back to a unified base. Its thesis first distinguishes in despair not to will to be oneself. It then emphasizes Kierkegaard's insight that the complementary willing to be oneself means: we want to be what we are not. But it also calls for consideration that the reciprocal reducibility of the two forms of authentic despair asserted by Kierkegaard comes up against its limit in an asymmetry that attests to the priority of the not willing to be oneself. That is, while it invariably holds that we want to be what we are not because we do not want to be what we are, it is by no means always the case that we do not want to be what we are because we want to be

what we are not. Finally, the thesis discloses the not willing to be oneself even in inauthentic despair. Not to be conscious of having a self—that means on the level on which Kierkegaard starts off: not even to begin to establish oneself in a relation of denial or acceptance to one's Dasein. Therein lies, in turn, its own kind of not willing, one in which an act of willing does not even occur, neither the positive willing nor the not willing as willing in the mode of negation. Kierkegaard goes beyond the purview of his basic proposition only at the end of his course through the forms of consciousness, where he focuses on a despairing willing to be a self that has a different structure than the not willing to be what one is not, but that can only be understood theologically, as a revolt against a God, against whom the person in despair wants to be himself in such a way that he derides Him, in a kind of perversion of not being in despair. Nowhere does the course through the forms into which the failure to accomplish the synthesis of being human solidifies leave the space marked out at the beginning. He formulates the fundamental connection emanating from the basic proposition—which the philosophical consideration of consciousness divides into a sequence of stages—as an order of priority in the logical-ontological construction of failing existence: we do not want to be what we are as humans and we therefore want to be what as humans we are not.

Deducing Kierkegaard's analysis of despair from a single principle was a work of reconstruction. From the work of reconstruction, which by and large has been accomplished, we not only demarcated the task which our study at least tackled toward the end: that of defining the place of *The Sickness unto Death* within the context of the history of human self-understanding. In addition, two research areas emerged, whose treatment remains a desideratum: the problematization of the premise that was designated fundamental and a critique, which in contrast to the immanent critique implicit in the reconstruction itself, may be called transcending. The premise of Kierkegaard's analysis of despair that we exposed is to be examined in terms of the question of whether we really do not want to be what we are and, in if this holds true, why do we not want to be what we are. Kierkegaard himself is apparently so certain that it holds true that he is only interested in the "why," and even to the question of "why," he explicitly gives only a theological answer: we do not want to be what we are because we are in the state of sin.[1] In doing that, he describes the same figure of despair as in his *philosophy* of despair. He finds his answer by resorting to a depth level of the concept of sin as developed from the myth of original sin. That we want to be God means: we want to be what we are not, but that is because we do not want to be what we are. To get beyond the theological answer, we need only get into the historical situation to which Kierkegaard's philosophy of despair is reacting. In *Either/Or*, the concept of despair was an interpretative category for the nihilism heralded by German Romanticism.[2] We do not want to be what we are because with being having become void, our own being has also become void from the very beginning and, in this very voidness, unacceptable for us. Yet the nihilistic connotations of the concept of despair manifest themselves only by way of a transcending critique. Such a critique not only has to examine whether the interpretation given by this concept of despair does justice to the nihilistic experiences of loss. It must also be open to which the possibility that nihilism informs the interpretation to which Kierkegaard subjects despair. First of all, the plan of a transcending critique is to be outlined more precisely.

2. The claim that Kierkegaard subjects despair to an interpretation implies that he is not content with pure description. We do owe him a genuine phenomenological insight into the matter. But in *The Sickness unto Death*, the attempts at a phenomenology of despair have to fend off a constructivist theory. Kierkegaard relies primarily on the consistency of thought, with the assumption, still close to idealism, that it is consistency that

guarantees accuracy.³ In truth, the interpretation not only discloses; it also closes *off*. And it closes off in a twofold way. On the one hand, contrary to its own self-conception, it does not capture everything about despair. On the other hand, it apprehends a good many things which, on closer inspection, are not despair. In one respect, it impoverishes the phenomenon; in the latter respect, it enriches it with alien supplements. Accordingly, a transcending critique must observe the double function, on the one hand, to clear what has been made unfamiliar from what has been added from outside and, on the other hand, to reimburse what has been impoverished with what has been excised from it. The critique is productive especially in the latter sense. However, it does not become productive by bringing something external to bear on its subject matter. At least in our present case, it may take up the self-transcending acts of the theory under discussion. For these self-transcending acts, there is a relatively unambiguous criterion in *The Sickness unto Death*. They are indicated by the appearance of so-called unannounced facts. It is conspicuous in Kierkegaard's treatise on despair that, amid remarks that ostensibly serve nothing but the development of its approach, it comes up against facts that were not foreseen by that approach. As early as the last part of A, the initial distinctions are joined by one whose relation to them remains obscure: the distinction between despair over something and despair over oneself.⁴ It advances to being the central topic in the passage devoted to the despair of weakness,⁵ even though, according to the outline of the treatise, this passage is only supposed to explain what it means, concretely, in despair not to will to be oneself. This is curious chiefly because the new topic can hardly be dismissed as being secondary to the one presented initially. On the contrary, it assumes a fundamental status. Consequently, it enters into competition with the initial approach. In this context, it is irrelevant for the moment whether Kierkegaard himself thinks—as he does with respect to the despair over oneself—he has something fundamental in mind or whether he dismisses the fundamental claim, as he does in the despair over something. It is precisely the emphasis with which he ostensibly seeks to dissolve the originality of despair over something that reveals how powerfully the facts emerging unannounced break into his prefabricated schema. Here as there, he reacts to the confrontation with aspects that are suppressed by his approach, here by repressing them, there by acknowledging them. The case at hand compels him not only toward acknowledgment but also toward repression. The difference is that, in the one case, it is an achieved self-transcendence of the theory; in the other, one that simply happens; and what the transcending critique, for its part, can use as its vehicle in the one case, it still has to make its subject in the other.

At the same time, the self-transcending acts of the theory which materialize all the same point to the direction in which the critique connected with them has to seek its material. If the study that was concerned primarily with the initial approach was able—for the sake of the fundamental premise of the theory—to pursue its further steps on the line on which they secure the territory initially seized, now what is of interest is what is not on that line; and if the focus on the progress loyal to the line concerned only the external view that was granted by the edifice constructed on the foundation, now the orientation is guided by the deviant tendencies within the internal space of the later sections. First of all, we must gain access to the inside of the passage on the despair of weakness. But even before that, the goal of the transcending critique is to be envisaged. Such a critique is called for because Kierkegaard also gives an obstructing interpretation of despair. How does his interpretation obstruct? Why does it not get a grasp on everything about despair? And why does it extend to things that have little or nothing to do with despair?

What in that study is regarded as a "fundamental premise" of Kierkegaard's theory seems to be such only in the framework of the approach of his theory. One thing is certain: that we do not will to be what we are grounds our willing to be what we are not, as well as our ignorance of having a self. However, it looks as if there is an even more elementary premise in this concept of inauthentic despair and in the corresponding conception of authentic despair, according to which the will of impossibility defining it is aimed at the person in despair, that is, the premise that all despair is enclosed within the circle of the relation to the self. Here, indeed, two premises may be differentiated: one that is within reach of an immanent critique and one that becomes fully accessible only to a transcending critique. The former is inherent in the theory, in the sense that on its own ground, alternatives to that theory are conceivable; whereas the latter, insofar as it is virtually without alternative for the producer of the theory, occupies a meta-theoretical status. However, whether the second is a more elementary premise vis-à-vis the first is not the only question to be settled; we must also ask whether Kierkegaard, with his orientation to the self, makes a premise at all. The assertion that according to his own conception, all despair is enclosed within the circle of self-relation, uses a vague metaphor. It is a pressing task fully to differentiate the image in conceptual terms. The premise-like character and the status of what is undoubtedly the deepest of all convictions guiding the author of *The Sickness unto Death* will evolve from our conceptual work.

In Kierkegaard's view, the self-relation of despair is based first and foremost on the fact that it always arises from the person in despair, regardless of what that person may trace his despair back to.[6] Therefore, as it says in *The Sickness unto Death*, the outside can at most be an occasion for our being in despair, but never its source that, rather, has to be the so-called self. In any case, this assumption goes beyond a mere premise if by that we understand a thesis which is implausible prima facie and therefore may function only as a *hypo*thesis until it is verified. For, as will be shown in detail, it is evident that despair at least *also* arises from the subject. A presupposition in the sense of an implausible supposition only consists in the idea that despair arises *only* from the subject. This is confirmed by authentic despair, in which the source becomes the subject matter. An adequate consciousness of the despair arising from the self evolves only—according to its diagnostician—if the person in despair reflects on himself. Even such a statement is valid, with the qualification that it is wrong as soon as it is linked with the view that, to be aware of his condition, the person in despair needs to reflect on nothing but himself. Incidentally, the concrete self-relation, which characterizes authentic despair per se, must not be confused with the self-relation which characterizes the despair over oneself mentioned above, a special form of authentic despair. Kierkegaard's talk of a despair over oneself is fraught with a variety of equivocations. He can assert the originality of this form of despair[7] only because he traces it back to a completely different one. In fact, despair over oneself coincides with the despair that objectifies its source in that it, too, is not immediate despair but constitutes an advanced stage in the subject's history of suffering, still to be classified more precisely. But if I may again express myself metaphorically, the two forms of despair are written into the self-relation in an entirely different manner. The despairing person or, more precisely, the person in despair who recognizes himself as a source of his condition relates to himself in a way that is itself not in despair. For, by becoming aware of himself, he takes a first step on the path that can lead to his healing. The person who despairs over himself, on the other hand, has a self-relation that is beset by his despair. But the desperation of his relation to himself is nothing peculiar only to him. What is peculiar to him consists merely of the desperation of that which he relates to in despair. According to Kierkegaard, that the self-relation as such is in despair constitutes the original fact in any despair, in every authentic as well as in every inauthentic despair. That factum is in principle not identical with the fact that all despair has its source in the self, but does belong with it. Both define the sense in which it can be said that, for Kierkegaard, all despair is enclosed within the circle of self-relation. Thus, both also constitute the content of the newly envisaged premise. Therefore, there is no more reason to suppose that the thesis about the fundamental desperation of the self-relation breaks down into a pure premise than there is reason to suppose the assessment that all despair originates in the self does. No despair seems to be possible without the desperation of the self-relation, even if it is more than what is lodged in it.

To some extent, Kierkegaard's interpretation already closes off the phenomenon by reducing despair to the desperation of the self-relation. It closes it off doubly in the way described by excluding everything to do with despair that goes beyond the desperation of the self-relation and by including a deficiency of the self's relating to itself, which is not really despair. For, strictly speaking, that is, Kierkegaard does not even start with despair but with such a deficiency, namely such that he also subsumes its not-despaired instantiations under despair.[8] Even so, he reduces the deficient self-relation as far as that is concerned. He limits it initially to willing and then to being, that is, to willing to be and its negation. This is proved by the result reached by the immanent critique of his doctrine of the failure to accomplish that synthesis that constitutes being human. Even if the failure to accomplish that synthesis is caused by the fact that we do not will to be what we are as humans and therefore will to be what as humans we are not, there is, according to Kierkegaard, no relating to oneself in despair or considered to be in despair that would be anything other than this willing to be or willing not to be. The desperation of the relation to oneself coincides with the fact that one wills in despair to be oneself or wills in despair not to be oneself. More precisely: it is only what it is, real desperation, as long as it can be shown to be the desperation of to will or not to will to be oneself, that of a willing which—as a willing of what is impossible to obtain—is undoubtedly in despair.

We are now in a position to answer the still open question of whether the premise of the transcending critique is more elementary than the one exposed in the immanent critique. If the self-relation, to whose desperation Kierkegaard reduces all despair, can for its part be traced back to that desperation he explicates in terms of being and willing, then the self-relation may be traced back even further to the one which the desperation explained in terms of being and willing, may be reduced, that is, to the fact that in despair we do not will to be what we are. In this respect, the premise that despair is at home in the self-relation and nowhere else is not more elementary than the premise Kierkegaard makes by starting with this not willing to be. In another sense, however, it is more elementary indeed. It is more elementary on the level of a pre-understanding that has, always already, marked out the only field in which substantive decisions can be made, including the decision for the primacy of not willing to be. This decision is already preceded by the decision to admit to the competition for primacy only forms of self-relation that are deficient because the called-for willing to be does not materialize. To be sure, in no case does a malformed relation to oneself suffice for admission. Rather, it must also be able to be identified as a failure to comply with the demand for willing to be. Linguistically, the admission criteria can be read in both forms of authentic despair, in whose definition none of the three elements of "self," "being," and "willing" may be lacking. But even inauthentic despair must submit completely to the conditions of the competition. The last two elements of the definition are not represented in their linguistic versions only because Kierkegaard does not define them through the first, either, but rather through the "self." Their re-definition also exposes them as a form of not willing to be.

Now, by reducing the self-relation's deficiency to the absence of the called-for willing to be, it is emptied even beyond the measure that, taken for itself, it is already in. The emptying mainly affects the properly functioning self-relation and from there bears upon the dysfunctional self-relation. On closer inspection, it occurs with the second step of the reduction of the self-relation, with the reduction of willing to the willing of one's own being. A certain emptiness spreads already as the postulate of willing to be oneself refers everyone back to himself, insofar as it commits us to nothing but what is, in each case, one's own. But the emptiness spreads even further because this postulate, precisely by restrictively defining willing as willing to be, calls for nothing but the execution of what is, in each case, one's own. To be sure, the substantive does not yet disappear so completely as it does in an existential ontology, for which Dasein in each case has to be its being as its own. But it does not yet disappear completely only because what is to be executed is *what* we are, and not, by contrast, pure being. That being that is assigned to be the immediate object of willing, the existential consummation of what is pre-given to ourselves in substantive determinateness, is—as execution—itself ontological, that is, aside from its religious filling, it is absolutely empty.

3. This finding feeds the suspicion expressed above that Kierkegaard reproduces the nihilism he interprets as despair in its own interpretation. He seems to reproduce it by evaluating despair according to the criterion of a willing to be oneself, which, in its emptiness, is affected by nullity. However, it would be naïve to accuse him of that. If his philosophy of despair does indeed respond to a nihilism that prevails objectively in his historical situation, then it was not even possible to keep its projection of an alternative to the existence in despair free of nihilistic experiences. In the concluding part of the study on the "fundamental principle" of this philosophy, *The Sickness unto Death* was placed at the beginning of an epoch which no longer calls on men to realize a definition of man, as antiquity and the Middle Ages do, and can no longer appeal to a natural tendency to unfold our individuality, as early modernity does, but rather only calls for an individualization that precisely is not in our

natural tendency. But rejecting the idea of a definition of man did not originate in a subjective whim. It was enforced after it became doubtful whether a definition of man even existed, and if so, what it consisted of. The loss of a certain knowledge of the definition of man heralded the more universal loss of meaning, which found its most extreme expression in nihilism. The ethic that imposes on the individual the duty to execute his void Dasein against his immediate will takes this process seriously. The voidness of the willing to be that it postulates is the price demanded by its historical situation.

To be sure, Kierkegaard's historically situated interpretation burdens its transcending critique with a problem, which may not be ignored. An immanent critique can infer its criterion from the intentions with which it measures the factual execution of a theory. A transcending critique does not have such a criterion at its disposal. It receives its directive from its subject's view of the issue at hand. Therefore, it finds no access to the issue itself; it is incapable of applying an absolute criterion to its subject. But what, then, gives it the right? A proponent of classical phenomenology will retort that his approach to the phenomenon is not merely subjective because his essential insight does, after all, afford a privileged access to it. However, what is constitutive for the essential insight of phenomenology is the abstraction from history. Consequently, it may not be invoked by the transcending critique in the present case. That is, it is hardly possible for our intended critique here to confront Kierkegaard's historically situated interpretation with a metahistorical view of the issue. It would probably be unable to do that even if it were able to cleanse its guiding view of the particularities of its subject. For the phenomenon of which Kierkegaard gives a historically situated interpretation presumably is itself historically determined. If this were in fact the case, we would have to assume that it would remain historically determined even if it were cleansed of its particular subjectivity. And then it would be inconceivable for the conception claiming to correct Kierkegaard's interpretation to rise above the level of an interpretation, which, in its act of disclosing, closes off at the same time. Last but not least, the historicity of a phenomenon after all consists in the fact that it is given only as being, always already, interpreted. It is precisely for this reason that any essential insight claiming to be free of history and thus free of interpretation must fail.

This aporia can be solved not by disregarding history, but only through an unconditional acknowledgment of it. No doubt we would not even get into this aporia if the assumption that the phenomenon under discussion is itself historical were unwarranted. Indeed, its historicity does not necessarily follow from that the fact that, in formulating his philosophy of despair, Kierkegaard reacts to a historically given nihilism. After all, he could have explicated a historical phenomenon in meta-historical terms. Thus, whether the concept of despair itself includes history is to be examined independent of its use as an interpretive category for nihilism. As long as it is not examined, the assertion of its historicity has no more evidence than the assertion of its meta-historicity. On closer inspection, however, it becomes obvious quite quickly that the concept of despair is historical even in the strictest sense. If something is historical at all, it can be thus in either an accidental or substantial, partial, or total way. Furthermore, it can participate in history in the sense that it has always already existed, but only in a different way each time, or such that at one point it did not exist at all and came into being only at a certain point in time. Clearly, something that is completely suffused with history is historical in a stricter sense than something that withdraws from it, and something that comes into being in history is historical in an even stricter sense than something that merely changes within it. Now, within the history that the concept of despair was subject to, there is a caesura that looks like a fracture, at least at first glance. I mean the change from *desperatio* to despair in the specific meaning of the German (and Danish) word.[9] This was an essential change. Because the issue received another point of reference, doubt instead of hope, it turned into something else, especially since the relation was restructured at the same time.[10]

For the relation of *desperatio* to *spes* is one of privation, whereas despair relates to doubt as the whole to the part; doubt becomes despair through a totalization.[11] Indeed, within the change something identical is maintained. Just as it will be shown that even the despair that totalizes doubt amounts to a loss of hope, so, in turn, does the *desperatio* exhibit a totalizing aspect. It implies that one lets go of *all* hope. Without an identical substance of meaning, we would hardly be able to translate the German (and Danish) word into the modern languages in which Latin survives. But what remains identical nonetheless assumes different connotations in particular constellations.

The change of essence indicated is so far-reaching that it must be taken into account when we ask whether despair exists always already or only from a certain time. What Kierkegaard means by *fortvivelse* can exist only under conditions that allow for a totalization of doubt. Thus, it presupposes Christianity. If totalized, doubt is the opposite of faith in the Christian understanding, of a faith that risks everything. It is precisely as a negation of such faith that it is linked to an epoch that is already open to the possibility of belief in reaching out to the whole. The paradigm shift within the history of the concept only reflects the radical change in real history effected by Christianity. Presumably, the phenomenon of the Latin word is not much older than the word itself. Early Hellenism confronts hope not with hopelessness but with its own defective forms, a void or vain or blind hope. How inconceivable hopelessness was to the early Greeks is shown by the example of a saying from the collection of Theognis that hope stays with us as the sole goddess after the other divinities have left us.[12] The element in *desperatio* that eluded archaic thinking was clearly the totalization appearing on the horizon. The despair that totalizes doubt would accordingly have been even more alien to this thinking.[13] For the totalizing aspect came to the fore as soon as *desperatio* turned into despair as understood verbatim.

Now it can be said with good reason that Kierkegaard totalizes even the totalization itself. That is, in his view, despair not only totalizes doubt. As we shall see, it totalizes everything, namely in such way that it is only in totalizing that it constitutes itself as what it is.[14] As a result, Kierkegaard's *forvivelse* is even more than a negation of faith rooted in the Christian terrain. Even beyond Christianity, it reflects nihilism. By using it, Kierkegaard does project an interpretive category that he applies to nihilism from outside. Rather, the nihilistic experiences to which its corresponding concept reacts are continued within it. Only because of that does Kierkegaard's interpretation have the chance to do justice to such experiences. And only because of that does its transcending critique have the chance of communicating with his interpretation rather than simply emphasizing a different conception of the phenomenon over against it. As a nihilistic experience itself, despair is a historical experience in itself. It is precisely because Kierkegaard interprets despair as a reflection of a historically determined nihilism that we can communicate with its interpretation, that is, understand it from within and also criticize it from within. As a medium of communication with this interpretation, a historical situation presents itself already which was his and still is ours. We can understand Kierkegaard's interpretation insofar as we also have nihilistic experiences, too; and we can criticize it in more ways from an outsider's point of view insofar as we are in principle capable of questioning it for its appropriateness for our own experiences.

II

1. The sketch of the project of a transcending critique has indicated where Kierkegaard's interpretation of despair transcends itself, especially the passage about the despair of weakness. The

problems visible in *The Sickness unto Death* from the perspective of a transcending critique can be summarized in one question: does its author succeed in integrating the despair of weakness into the process in which it—as the despair that lies in not willing to be oneself—turns into the despair of defiance, into in despair willing to be oneself? A critique that takes up the self-transcending elements of the text seeks to salvage the truth substance that we may grant it only to the extent to which the integration does *not* succeed.

The attempt at integration does in fact fail. The reason for its failure is also the reason why its failure can remain concealed. It resides in the ambiguity of the concept that Kierkegaard forms of what is to be integrated. That is, the weakness that is to mark not willing to be oneself also characterizes a suffering that is quite different from not willing to be oneself.[15] Kierkegaard definitely also subsumes the weakness under the suffering. But he is mistaken about its difference from not willing to be oneself because he apparently thinks that not to will to be oneself would constitute the form that comprises the diversity of what one suffers from as being itself identical.[16] That in reality we are dealing with two different forms of weakness is shown by a positive definition of suffering. In the despair of weakness, the despairing person suffers, as he conceives it, from what he is in despair about, on the one hand, and from his being in despair, on the other. Kierkegaard sometimes describes the one and sometimes the other as suffering, without working out the difference.[17] It is at least recorded in his language. It expresses the first suffering as an event plunging us into despair and marks the second by the phrase that despair itself overcomes us. But in both ways, his language testifies to a defined originality, the originality of an experience which as such is something that happens to, impinges on oneself.[18] Kierkegaard's official approach does not descend to this origin. A despair to which something bad has happened and which for that reason also happens itself is more original than one that merges into the execution of one's own Dasein and is more original than the most original mode of this deficiency, in despair not to will to be oneself. Of course, a willing also plays a part in it.[19] No one would fall into despair if what he does not want did not happen to him or if he were not denied what he wants. Likewise, he himself is involved. For in such a willing or not willing, he is concerned with himself. However, his despair need not lie at all in the desperation with which he wills or does not will *to be* himself. Rather, the desperation with which he does not will to be himself or, in abstracting from his facticity, wills to be himself, that is, really wills to be someone else, already presupposes a special variant of the despair happening to oneself: the despair that he is as he is.

The circumstance noted in the project outline, that our passage is essentially concerned with the initially disregarded despair over something and its metamorphosis, is to be seen against the background of the tension in the concept of its title. That Kierkegaard makes despair over something into the starting point of a passage whose subject is to be the despair of weakness reveals an involuntary admission of the priority of the weakness of suffering over the weakness of not willing to be oneself.[20] For behind despair over something lurks the happening despair over something that impinges on oneself. However, it itself is ambivalent. It was already ambivalent where it first appeared, in the last section of A, where Kierkegaard illustrates it with two examples. The only suitable example of an event happening to oneself that breaks the framework of in despair to will or not to will to be oneself is that of the young girl who despairs over the loss of her beloved.[21] To be precise, this example is also ambivalent in itself. Its ambivalence is reflected in that Kierkegaard again exemplifies the loss twofold, through death or unfaithfulness. In the case of unfaithfulness, the girl's despair does not go beyond her self-relation. A woman despairing over the unfaithfulness of her partner always despairs that *she* has lost something. In the case of death, on the other hand, the despair can break out of the self-relation. A woman despairing over the death of her partner may be in despair because *he* has lost something, namely, his life. Naturally, Kierkegaard does not consider this possibility. On the other hand, neither does he advance any arguments against it, least of all the argument of its incompatibility with the concept of despair. In truth, he excludes this possibility because, except for brotherly love conceived as duty without inclination, he cannot imagine any love that would not be self-love.[22] But it is for this reason that it does present itself to him within the horizon of his concept of despair, if only on the fringes, as it were, and independent of his subjective intention. It is precisely the objective presence of something that is enough to make one despair even without consideration of one's own ability to be that distinguishes this example from the others. Cesare Borgia also despairs over something, but only over something he cannot be. He despairs over the fact that he did not become Caesar. According to Kierkegaard, any despair over something turns into the despair it already was in itself: into despair over oneself. In the case of Cesare Borgia, that means in despair over not having become Caesar, he despairs over himself as someone who is such that he could not become Caesar.[23] This despair is encompassed completely by the desperation of willing and not willing to be oneself. What it amounts to is that Cesare Borgia despairingly does not will to be himself, and it springs from the fact that he just as despairingly wanted to be himself, that is, a person who he is not, and his so-called willing to be himself is again based on the fact that, from the very beginning, he did not want to be himself, that is, the person he is. Insofar as Kierkegaard orients himself toward the maxim of *Aut Caesar aut nihil*, he also forces the despair over something to submit to the rule of in despair not to will to be oneself.[24]

Kierkegaard can neutralize the ambiguity that characterizes despair over something—insofar as it oscillates between the weakness of not willing to be oneself and the weakness of suffering—only by accepting another ambivalence. According to A, despairing over something is not yet despair proper.[25] This contradicts the fact that the despair over something, explained only with examples in A, is developed conceptually in the context of the discussion of in despair not to will to be oneself. For this is a form and is in fact the basic form of authentic despair. This contradiction can hardly be resolved by contrasting the "not yet" authentic despair with inauthentic despair. For the despair over something is characterized in the same way as inauthentic despair so that in it the person is neither aware of himself nor of it and has no consciousness of it, insofar as he neither knows what it is in itself nor realizes that he is in a condition of despair.[26] The new ambiguity can be contained only by identifying—behind Kierkegaard's back, as it were—the despair over something, which in his estimation is an inauthentic despair, as the happening despair over something that impinges on one, and by identifying the authentic despair as the despair with which, as in the case of Cesare Borgia, the actualization of the basically already prevailing not willing to be oneself begins. However, limiting inauthentic despair over something to the weakness of suffering does not exempt us from the task of outlining a distinction that is leveled by subsuming inauthentic despair over something under the essential definition of inauthentic despair proper. A person who despairs over something that happens to him cannot lack a consciousness of his despair in the same way as the person whose despair has thus far been deemed inauthentic. The former is not aware of his despair at all, whereas the latter merely lacks a consciousness of what despair really is. For, while the former, according to Kierkegaard, lives in real despair without thinking he is in despair, the latter is overcome by merely putative despair, that is, one that really is not despair.[27] In the former, not to be in despair is mere semblance; in the latter, it is being in despair. Kierkegaard's attempt to dissolve despair over something into appearance is in line with a strategy that aims at exposing the talk of a happening despair as meaningless and at tracing it back to a self-misunderstanding.[28] But to inform an unhappy person who thinks he is in despair that he is not is just as questionable as demonstrating to a happy person who thinks he is not in despair that he is. Inasmuch as Kierkegaard fancies himself in the role of the physician who thinks he can diagnose an illness without considering the subjective opinion of the patient, his diagnosis can be nothing but an external classification in terms of a prefabricated concept.[29] That is, he has no criteria available for his judgment on the seeming nature of being and not being in despair that would be independent of his definition of despair as a deficiency of a self-relation reduced to the execution of one's own Dasein.

The only thing plausible in all that may be that the allegedly seeming and in that sense inauthentic despair over something can have nothing to do with the fact that one despairingly does not will to be oneself. For whoever does not want to be himself is in real despair. Now, one should expect that Kierkegaard acknowledges the kind of despair that appears on the horizon of in despair not willing to be oneself as real despair. Yet this expectation is disappointed. Kierkegaard attributes every despair over something that is despair only in the consciousness of the despairing person to mere semblance. Hence, it must be concluded: the tension between the weakness equated in the title of the passage with the basic form of authentic despair is even more far-reaching than was supposed. It is not only that the weakness inherent in not willing to be oneself must share its place with a differently composed weakness of suffering. Instead, it does not even appear at the beginning of the passage. As long as Kierkegaard follows the main theme of despair over something, it must leave the field to its rival. It only appears with the progress toward a despair over oneself, whose concept has also changed completely vis-à-vis the last part of A. If Cesare Borgia despaired over himself because he did not get to become Caesar, to despair over oneself now means: to despair over one's weakness.[30] The despair over one's own weakness is supposed to prove that the immediate despair of weakness consisted in not willing to be oneself.[31] Indeed, it entails not willing to be oneself. Even if it does not coincide with it, it does follow from it. Anyone who despairs over the fact that he was weak enough to despair usually does not want to be the sort of weakling he is.[32] But it will not do to project not to will to be oneself back onto the immediate despair of weakness. For the basic form of authentic despair presupposes exactly the kind of reflection that the immediate despair of weakness does not yet muster. The sequence of immediate and reflected despair of weakness virtually affords involuntary evidence that the desperation with which someone does not or does will to be himself refers to a more original despair. In addition, it deserves to be emphasized that the reflected form is not identical with the basic form of authentic despair. It cannot be the case that the initially suppressed weakness of not willing to be oneself itself suppresses the weakness of suffering. For the person despairing over his weakness does not only entrench himself *in* his weakness; he deepens the weakness itself, and he deepens it as what it was from the beginning, a weakness of suffering. In advancing to despair over one's weakness, Kierkegaard shifts even despair over oneself into the perspective of despair originally happening to oneself.

2. Between the immediate despair of weakness and that of defiance, the despair over one's own weakness seems to be merely an interim stage. In truth, it is the axis around which everything revolves. It gains an axial position because of its strategic function. Its task, to commit the despair in weakness to a not willing to be oneself for which there were no direct signs, constitutes only part of this function. On the other hand, it serves the purpose of finding the despair of weakness guilty of defiance.[33] In this respect, it has great significance for Kierkegaard's overall strategy of a dialectic mediation of the opposition of weakness and defiance. With the consequence of his thesis of the recipro-

cal reducibility of both forms, Kierkegaard's overall aim is to evince an element of defiance in weakness and an element of weakness in defiance. In his plan, what is initially of interest is the former, the proof of an element of defiance in weakness. Kierkegaard already tries to turn this defiance into not willing to be oneself by direct access, that is, even before its interpretation as weakness. The study of the fundamental principle of the analysis of despair presented in *The Sickness unto Death* demonstrated that the author does not succeed—by way of this proof—in grounding the not willing to be oneself in the willing to be oneself. Since defiance is tied, as arrogance of self-construction, to what is illegitimately called willing to be oneself, that is, to the willing to be what we are not, and since it is just as impossible to extract the rebellious defiance from the despair of the person who in fact wants to be himself in order to disavow his Creator, Kierkegaard can only claim a third mode of defiance, the defiance of despairingly willing the impossible, which, however—as a mode that comprises both forms of despair—does not surrender the not willing to be oneself to the willing to be oneself. To be sure, this implies that Kierkegaard is indeed able to demonstrate an element of defiance in not willing to be oneself. Thus, at the beginning of the passage about the despair in weakness, he also seems to come back to the defiance of willing the impossible. However, from there, he does not get one step beyond the weakness of not willing to be oneself. In the weakness of suffering, he finds no trace of defiance.

The limits set for defiance in its weakness become clearer when we confront the despair over one's own weakness and ask the question of how and to what extent it fulfills its own function of disclosure. In the immediate despair in weakness, no defiance can be seen because it has nothing yet of in despair not to will to be oneself. On the other hand, we have seen that such not willing to be oneself can at least follow from the despair over one's own weakness. Accordingly, something like defiance emerges only in its wake. Kierkegaard appeals to its lack of humility.[34] But a lack of humility is betrayed only by a person who, out of despair over his weakness, does not will to be himself. Moreover, it may of course be questionable whether a lack of humility must be defiance.

Here the same doubt appears that is already evoked by the way Kierkegaard takes up the idea of defiantly willing the impossible at the beginning of the passage. In his search for the element of defiance in weakness, Kierkegaard turns to a not willing to be which, to be precise, is something more universal than not willing to be *oneself*.[35] In this respect, we might think he does not even appeal to defiantly willing the impossible. After all, what was impossible was not to be oneself. On the other hand, it would be perfectly possible not to be at all. If Kierkegaard actually sought defiance in a more universal not willing to be and if it were also assumed that he finds what he is looking for, then regarding the point in question, we would get considerably beyond the study of the fundamental premise of his analysis. For then we would have to consider a fourth mode of defiance which specifically suits in despair not to will to be oneself, not merely as a result of its agreement with in despair to will to be oneself. Even in that case, there would be no reason to correct the result of that study. For the new form of defiance cannot be claimed for grounding the despaired not willing to be oneself in the despairing willing to be oneself any more than the defiance of willing the impossible can. If defiance is inherent in not willing to be, even before its specification as not willing to be oneself, then it indeed precedes the willing to be oneself. To be sure, it would produce the proof that not to will to be oneself, just like not willing to be, implies its own kind of defiance. However, defiance is heard in the expression "not to will to be" only in a certain pitch. A necessary condition for that would be that a tone of rejection resonates in the expression. Obviously there is a not wanting that is not a rejecting. It is precisely as a despairing not willing that it will in the fewest cases be backed by an attitude of rejection. And even if it were to reject, it still would not fulfill a sufficient condition for defiance. For not every rejection is defiant. Defiance presupposes a certain unreasonableness. Someone who reasonably rejects something does not therefore behave defiantly. On balance: that not to will to be oneself contains an element of defiance does not hold in terms of the universality claimed by Kierkegaard.

Thus it is shown that the validity of the whole theory about the defiance in weakness is limited to an extremely narrow area. The weakness of suffering lacks defiance entirely, and defiance penetrates the weakness of not willing to be oneself only under special circumstances. Someone who out of despair over his weakness does not will to be himself—and only that person represents in our passage the second type of weakness—certainly refrains from humbling himself under his weakness. But as long as he does not commit a sin entirely different from this sin of omission, he is very far from turning his weakness into defiance.

3. In Kierkegaard's attempt to demonstrate an element of defiance in weakness and an element of weakness in defiance, we shall now be concerned with the latter, the proof of an element of weakness in defiance.[36] That defiance reveals weakness is intuitively plausible, even if otherwise it presupposes a certain unreasonableness. However, Kierkegaard almost over-fulfills the task he set for himself of finding even despair guilty of weakness. For he fulfills this task in such a way that turns his own conception of despair on its head. It is enough to look at the organization of the passage about the despair of defiance to see that. It is based on the distinction between an acting and a self acted on.[37] This distinction becomes the organizing principle since Kierkegaard also derives from it the right to separate defiant despair, too, into an acting and a suffering one. By that, however, he shifts the comprehensive difference between despair of weakness and despair of defiance inside the latter. If such an operation must endanger the consistency of a theory

conclusively aiming to reduce everything to the defiance that is weak only in its own way, then the theory's approach reveals its own real destruction, when we consider how and where the theory smuggles the despair of weakness into that of defiance. That is, in accordance with the idea of a suffering self it is the weakness of suffering that recurs in defiance, and it recurs in the most extreme defiance. It is not the self acted on that is supposed to change into an acting self, but rather, vice versa, the acting self is to turn into a suffering one. Along with Hegel, Kierkegaard conceives of the completion of despair in defiance in such a way that elucidates this: basically, defiance constituted the beginning as well. As for defiant despair, if it completes itself in the weakness of suffering, then—according to the logic of the concept of the end as the developed beginning—the originality exactly follows the despair which stands in an unmediated opposition to it. The final stage of the process that despair goes through on the path of its intensification confirms the interpretation which claims that this process began with an original suffering.

Naturally, Kierkegaard can only reluctantly allow the return of the weakness of suffering. If it is correct that weakness thus defined, unlike the weakness of not willing to be oneself, does not contain even a seed of defiance, then it excludes conclusively the fully developed defiance. But Kierkegaard must *allow* its return. For it owes its return not to any external organizing principle. Rather, it intrudes because without it, fully developed defiance would remain inconceivable. By means of the distinction between an acting self and a self acted on, Kierkegaard marks the split separating arrogant and rebellious defiance from one another. Under the rubric of the acting self, he reformulates in despair to will to be oneself in the form in which it was introduced, as an experimenting willing to be what factically one is not, and one merely appropriates in an arrogant construction. The suffering self, on the other hand, is the self of the person who wills to be himself in the strict sense that through defiantly fixating on himself, he revolts against his Creator, and finally—in the demonic nature of his despair—forces himself on him. But such a person is suffering because he has discovered a difficulty in his existence which he cannot master and which thus ruins his joy in experimenting.[38] Only as a result of this discovery does the arrogant defiance become rebellious. Thus, defiance is only a—and by no means necessary—reaction to suffering. This means that the despair of defiance is preceded by a completely different one, the despair over the distress on which all experimenting founders.[39] It is the despair in whose weakness returns the original weakness of suffering. To be sure, the suffering remains unconceptualized in Kierkegaard. It disappears behind defiance, which compensates for it. It is only because it is suppressed that we may explain why Kierkegaard does not note the contradiction in which he gets entangled when he designates the person whose rebellious gesture is the opposite of suffering nonetheless as suffering.[40]

4. In sum, the examination of the thesis of a mutual implication of weakness and defiance has shown an asymmetry in the relation of the two components that is reminiscent of the asymmetric relation of in despair not to will to be oneself and in despair to will to be oneself. Just as not to will to be oneself takes primacy over a willing to be that is in despair only in other ways, so weakness takes precedence over defiance. Since Kierkegaard merely translates the conceptual pair introduced right at the beginning of *The Sickness unto Death* into the later one, the analogy should hardly come as a surprise. What is more remarkable are its limitations. For a difficulty of translation is revealed in them. The new asymmetry is based essentially on a difference of status between the element of defiance in weakness and the element of weakness in defiance. Weakness contains a merely accidental element of defiance, which is not found at all in the weakness of suffering and which even in the weakness of not willing to be oneself is limited to particular forms of manifesta-

tion. Defiance, on the other hand, refers back to a weakness that is actually more than an element, that is, to the substantial basis from which it leaps off so that it is only in leaping off that it actually becomes what it is. Nonetheless, the implied elements do have something in common: they are both beyond the framework that contains the asymmetry of the forms of despair that is articulated with the help of the first conceptual pair. The defiance in weakness goes beyond the self-relation internally, as it were. That, at any rate, would have to be said if the difference between not willing to be and not willing to be *oneself* is to be more than just verbal. The weakness in defiance transcends the self-relation externally. For it manifests itself in something that, while it belongs to one's own Dasein, happens to the subject even before he relates to it. After all, the subject relates to the distress in his Dasein in such a way that he merely reacts to it, that is, in defiance.

This is ignored by the discussion of defiance in weakness and weakness in defiance. It covers up the fact that defiance implies a weakness other than the one that implies defiance. Ultimately, the failure of the project of a dialectical mediation of the opposition is thus covered up. Under the conditions created by the translation of the first conceptual pair into the second one, the project must fail because it presupposes the semantic identity of the terms to be mediated. In the relation of weakness and defiance, moreover, the implied and the implying also diverge in that, in terms of its meaning, the implying defiance is different from the implied as well. The defiance of rejection is contrasted with a defiance which, to be precise, does not reject but accepts. This too bursts the framework of the old asymmetry. With accepting defiance, the correctly called willing to be oneself enters the scene, which was not included in the comparison of the forms of despair examined in terms of their reciprocal reducibility. But what is significant for a transcending critique is the appearance of the weakness of suffering. For with that, what is negative—the failure of a theory seeking to capture defiance in the circle of the dialectic of willing to be oneself and not willing to be oneself—is revealed as something positive: the self-transcending of this theory. More precisely, what is significant is that a weakness that initially escapes the process of mediation eventually appears as a weakness that mediates both—the weakness of not willing to be oneself and the defiance of willing to be oneself—with its ground.

III

1. In all preceding considerations, one thing only was presupposed: that the weakness of suffering was free of defiance. The premise can be justified only if we take into account a previously ignored operation that plays a considerable role in the analyzed attempt of an exposure of defiance in weakness: Kierkegaard formalizes defiance into the principle of self-activity per se.[41] The operation is clearly based on the idea that manifest defiance requires the most extreme activity from the subject and that therefore a latent defiance must already reside in any less extreme action. Thus, Kierkegaard himself provides the argument for the freedom of the happening despair out of defiance. If what happens to one is a pure suffering then it cannot be acting and consequently cannot even contain one grain of defiance in itself. We can simplify the argument in such a way that it also is plausible to us. Surely, no one will want to expand the concept of defiance into all action. As in most such operations, here, too, formalization makes the issue unrecognizable. However, what remains unaffected by that is the part of the idea that manifest defiance has amassed a considerable energy for action. What is defiant about despair invariably manifests itself conspicuously in a despaired act. It is true that the desperation of a despaired act is distinguished by the specific defiance in which one wills the impossible in the awareness of its impossibility. It is because a despaired act exhibits this specific defiance that the

act happens not only because one despairingly wills to be oneself. It may also burst out of the despair of the person who does not will to be himself, always, that is, when he translates his wish to get rid of himself into action, without necessarily committing suicide. But even in those who will to be what they are not by arbitrarily reconstructing their existence or in those who will to be what they are in a perverted fashion, as living proof against the power and goodness of their God, defiance manifests itself with a strange energy. By contrast, in a despair whose weakness is that of suffering, none of that kind of energy is to be found.

It is important to see that simplifying the argument frees the understanding of this despair from the premise that it is pure suffering. We would have to identify it as pure suffering only if we tried to acquit despair of the suspicion of defiance, and thus argued against Kierkegaard that, like him, we also thought that even the slightest activity would already succumb to defiance. If all that is needed for an acquittal is the insight that despair does not exhibit any increased activity, then there is no need to insist on the purity of suffering. It is important to see that, because otherwise it would easily seem as if a transcending critique that advances a weakness of suffering free of defiance, against Kierkegaard, comes merely from outside, and as such it could not be productive. Thus far, it may have given the impression that it was aimed against a false position per se, against which an abstract alternative had to be mobilized. But it was exposed to such a suspicion because the position taken by Kierkegaard has not yet divulged its truth content. The position criticized is only now to be recognized as correct. For the truth of Kierkegaard's concept of despair—independent of the adventurous conclusion he draws for defiance—lies in the assumption that any despair is an act. The truth content of this assumption shows itself even where Kierkegaard operates with it to expose the despair of weakness as a so-called embryonic despair of defiance. As we know, he seeks to reach his goal through the reflection of weakness, that is, through the despair in which weakness becomes the subject matter. In his view, despair over one's own weakness is already on its way to defiance, insofar as it brings to light that any despair comes from the self. The still unreflected despair of weakness is to come directly from outside, which we have to understand in such a way that, in it, the origin from the self is covered with the veil of unconsciousness. Defiance, by contrast, comes directly from the self. But the reflected despair of weakness anticipates it, as Kierkegaard asserts, by coming directly-indirectly from the self.[42] Leaving aside the dubious nature of the anticipation theorem, one plausible statement still remains. The term of a despair coming from the self is fraught with the metaphorical nature that was reproduced above in the discussion of Kierkegaard's conviction that any despair has its source in the self. The truth content of the theory is hidden in this conviction. To expose it, one need only dismantle the rampant metaphor. But stripped of its metaphor, Kierkegaard's fundamental conviction emerges in the form of his assumption that any despair is an act. The statement that any despair comes from the self or has its source in the self reveals its truth content as soon as it is given the form of the proposition that can be articulated conceptually: despair presupposes the self-activity of the person in despair.[43]

The truth content of the existential-dialectical concept of despair inherent in this recognition may, however, be secured only through a critique. For Kierkegaard puts himself in the wrong by making the active meaning of the phenomenon thoroughly absolute. He distorts it to pure acting. We would fall into the opposite extreme if, by contrast, we wanted to stylize the despairing that eludes subsumption under a defiant weakness as pure suffering. Despairing is neither a pure act nor pure suffering; it is both together. However, the asymmetry characteristic of the whole phenomenon appears here, too. Despairing never turns out to be a pure act. But in borderline situations, it can at least approach pure suffering. This is possible even in the limited territory of the dialectic of to will and not to will to be oneself. Despairing already tends to move toward pure suffering where we do not will to be what we are without willing to be what we are not. For here we lack the strength for an active projection of a fictive Dasein. If one were to turn a blind eye to such a tendency toward pure suffering, one would also have to deny the fact that the sickness of the spirit breaking out in the middle of everyday life, precisely because of a loss of self-activity, can lead to a mental illness to be treated clinically.[44] But Kierkegaard's error in making the aspect of activity absolute takes on more dubious forms, not only against the background of the asymmetry. It seems even worse in view of the coarse way Kierkegaard handles the concept of action itself. His formalization of defiance into the principle of all action continues, as it were, in its formalization. Or in other words: by making the active aspect of despair absolute, he brings in a preconception of action, which he makes absolute in turn. A critique seeking to fulfill the task mapped out in its name must therefore first separate Kierkegaard's legitimate use of the concept of action from his illegitimate use of this concept.

2. Everything in *The Sickness unto Death* that can claim unconditional agreement can be summed up in the proposition: anyone who despairs over something earthly makes this something, which is also always something particular, into the earthly *in toto*, and he could not do that if he did not live in despair of the eternal.[45] Every idea expressed in that proposition, even that of a despair of the eternal, is part of the inventory of the space opening within the analysis of weakness, which is hidden from the external perspective of a critique oriented to the schema of willing and not willing to be oneself. As for the idea of a despair of the eternal, it is especially solidly enclosed within this internal space: the crucial turn that Kierkegaard makes with it, the change from "despair over" to "despair of," is mainly made in an inconspicuous footnote.[46] The seclusion of the idea indicates

that it is not least this idea on which the truth content of the theory—which is first to be exposed—depends. However, for the time being, we may be content with thinking about the change of the word earthly into *the* earthly. For in this change, we encounter the act correctly ascribed to the phenomenon. One who despairs acts precisely by *making* this something into the whole. Here we confront the totalization that Kierkegaard expresses, insofar as he refers it not merely to doubt but to everything that can cause despair. His language indicates unmistakably that such an unlimited totalization is an essential part of any despair: it is already inherent in that we do not merely doubt (*zweifeln*) something, but despair (*verzweifeln*) over and of something. As the prefix indicates, despair would not even be possible without totalization. The act, regarded correctly, does not appear afterward; it is achieved in despairing. In this respect, it is naturally not an act, which as an act that becomes effective in the world had to be distinguished from pure activity. Nonetheless, we can appreciate that Kierkegaard calls it an act. Out of understandable interest in moral accountability, he gives it a name that presents the activity of despairing trenchantly as self-activity. The naming is to underscore that the definition of totality (*Totalitets-Bestemmelsen*) verbalized in the prefix of the word refers—precisely as a noetic definition—to an act of the despairing person, to a mental act. The despairing person acts insofar as he himself effects the fact that something particular takes on the appearance of the whole. And this is in fact the case: the totalization does not exist independent of him; it emerges only through totalization.

With his thesis about despair as a totalizing action, Kierkegaard establishes a criterion for the critique of his own theory. The distinction between something earthly and the earthly as such is made at the end of a section that previously treated the two subject matters of despair as if they were the same.[47] The totalization thesis does indeed imply a certain identity. According to this thesis, the belatedly marked difference would have to be grasped so that in fact despair over something earthly is always already despair over the earthly as such and is distinguished from it only because the despairing person does not yet know it as despair over the earthly as such. If to despair means to change something earthly into the earthly as such, then it cannot be grasped in its particularity. And yet it is despair over something that does the totalizing in this form. The reference to the earthly provides it only with an addition that is to classify it with the eternal. Consequently, even the despair over something is, objectively, already determined as an act. But it is precisely its active meaning that is denied by the verdict given it in *The Sickness unto Death*. For it dissolves into semblance because the pre-judgment prevails that it is not an act. Kierkegaard himself reduces despairing, as despairing over something, to pure suffering. Thus, he displays the background on which he unfolds the despair that is correlatively reduced to pure acting. In his own self-understanding, he naturally does not get involved in a contradiction with that thesis by reducing despair over something to pure suffering. He avoids the contradiction precisely by labeling it as merely putative. But to get out of the contradiction, he pays the price of not being able to acknowledge any real one in addition to the putative one. This means that he refuses to acknowledge precisely the despair claimed by his totalization thesis. In this respect, he does contradict himself. He gets entangled in the contradiction to affirm and negate a fact at the same time. The illegitimately excluded fact may be envisioned in his example of the young girl. According to *The Sickness unto Death*, the fact that a girl despairs over the death of her beloved implies in any case that her alleged despair is in truth only grief or something like that.[48] But the possibility that the girl is really in despair is not considered because she gives death an infinite significance. Thus Kierkegaard brushes aside what he himself presents: a despair that totalizes something earthly into the earthly as such.

The reason for this is that he evaluates despair over something according to the criterion of an illegitimate concept of action. Despair appears as a purely suffering despair, and as such it cannot be real because it lacks reflection, at least in the view of its diagnostician. Its reduction to pure suffering is thus based on the assumption that reflection is an act.[49] Kierkegaard thinks he even has to reserve the concept of action for reflection. He only *describes* the totalization as an act without drawing terminological consequences from that description. That the concept remains reserved for reflection obviously has strategic reasons. Its weight is to fall undivided on reflection because it has to bear the whole burden of proof of the advancing manifestation of defiance in all despair. The process of despair detailed in *The Sickness unto Death* is in fact only an advance in reflection. But Kierkegaard has to pass it off as an increasing conversion of suffering into action because he thinks he reaches his goal of exposing the defiance concealed in weakness via the detour through action. The case does not justify his procedure. Reflection in general is not action, least of all as reflection of despair. That is, in the process of despair, it leads to the opposite of action, to the intensification of suffering in oneself. Its reinterpretation as action thus turns the case of despair upside down.

However, Kierkegaard owes to his attention to reflection as such a certain correction of his polemic against despair over something. By reflection, which despair over something lacks completely in his view, he understands more closely the qualitative or infinite reflection, which is defined by the fact that it annuls immediacy. He distinguishes it from a quantitative or finite reflection, which deprives immediacy of its purity but does not put an absolute end to it. Despair over something, he concedes, is either pure immediacy or immediacy containing such a reflection.[50] But here, too, the truth may assert itself only against his intention. On the whole, Kierkegaard is convinced with Hegel that there is no pure immediacy.[51] If it is already incomprehensible that he now nevertheless asserts pure immediacy, then it borders on the absurd that of all things he encumbers a form of despair with it. Even a merely alleged despair excludes pure immediacy since it must at least be a kind of distress. To make any use of Kierkegaard's internal differentiation of despair over something earthly, it has to be modified to take pure immediacy as the construct of a background against which despair suffused with quantitative reflection stands out. Modified in this way, despair over something earthly would become legible as a mystified expression for a despair that has—always already, even as elementary despair over something—broken with pure immediacy, because as totalization it is an act of the subject. But Kierkegaard could hardly agree with such an interpretation. For by lowering the elementary despair over something to the level of pure immediacy, he proclaims his aim to keep the idea of a totalizing act far from it. And he absolutely does not want it to be understood as a concession to that despair itself that he allows it a transition to quantitative reflection. For, according to the authorized interpretation, despair over something becomes, through the quantity of reflection, a still incomplete despair over oneself. It is true that finite reflection is not a self-reflection in the strict sense in which infinite is; it is not a reflection of the self. But it does reveal parts of its own Dasein to the person. That Kierkegaard also interprets the reflection that elevates the happening despair over pure immediacy as a reversal of the despairing person to what causes despair in his own Dasein is suggested by a passage in which he apparently also enhances the status of a happening event. Anyone who talks about his despair over something earthly, says that passage, says something true, in a certain sense; but he is conversely situated and must literally be reversed.[52] Even his violent reversal is reflection, the external one that Kierkegaard makes for him. In an external reflection on his real despair, Kierkegaard reverses him so that he no longer has something in the world before himself, but rather himself. The violence of the measure illustrates how reflection carried out by the subject works, too: it substitutes something in the world with something in its own Dasein. Thus, that something that was the subject matter of happening despair disappears.

By entrusting reflection with the task of changing despair over something into despair over oneself, Kierkegaard unwittingly demonstrates the need for a critique of its confusion with activity. His assumption that reflection is an act is to be rejected not only because of its incompatibility with the issue at hand. It must also be rejected because it covers up the real activity of a despairing person. Kierkegaard's distinction between unreflected and reflected immediacy may at least be correct in that reflection is a supplement, even in the case of despair. To be sure, a self-presence of the subject is already part of the most immediate despair. But this self-presence is not yet reflection. And it is by no means the kind of reflection Kierkegaard has in mind here: one that makes out of despair over something a despair over oneself. The vagueness of that distinction follows not least from the fact that Kierkegaard really only thinks of it without naming it unequivocally. The reflection that changes despair over something into despair over oneself is fused with the reflection of the subject on itself taking place within despair over something of the subject. Here there is a return of the vagueness of the concept of inauthentic despair in which it remained unclear whether the subject has no consciousness of despair or of himself. But the reflection meant in fact comes, if it comes at all, even later than the one that is merely incidental. For a person can despair over himself only after he has become his own subject matter. If this reflection is now reinterpreted as an act and in addition so that an activity that is not reflection is denied, then the view of the real act performed by the despairing person from the start, even if he does not reflect it, is blocked. The reflection of the totalizing act really pushes the elementary despair beyond itself, indeed only to where it always already was: to the earthly in toto. But by blocking the totalizing act itself, Kierkegaard also gives away the chance to incorporate its reflection as the driving force in the process of despair. That he inserts the difference between despair over something earthly and despair over the earthly in toto only at the end of the section devoted to them—the difference that becomes clear only in this reflection—may be interpreted as an indication of the belief that he may leave both of them out of account in the treatment of his theme, the totalizing act and the driving reflection.

3. Kierkegaard's contradictory elimination—contradicting his own insight—of the active meaning from what for him is merely an ostensible despair occurs as a recoil from his making absolute the same meaning in the despair that is acknowledged as real. The primary thing is his conviction that a despair worthy of the name is *only* an act. That he does in fact have this conviction should have become plausible by now. His whole treatment of the phenomenon reveals that the energetic aspect is made absolute. It is only because he makes the element of activity into the whole that he can see in an exclusively active defiance the manifest secret of despair. But thus far it is not yet sufficiently demonstrated why Kierkegaard should not have the conviction that true despair emanates as an act. The antithesis—on which the right to criticize the move of making activity absolute depends—the claim that in the process of despairing, acting and suffering form a unity, is still shaky. We have certainly dealt sufficiently with the suffering in despair over something. Clearly, there is no disagreement about that. However, it cannot yet be taken for granted that the despair that Kierkegaard acknowledges as real and which he assumes—according to the contention of making it absolute—to be nothing but an act really does combine acting with suffering. To beat our opponent just where the dispute has flared up, we have to advance arguments against him that guarantee the asserted unity for *every* despair.

This task can also be accomplished by means of a critique that infers its criterion from what is criticized itself instead of applying its criterion from outside. If we argue with Kierkegaard, two arguments can be brought against him. It can be shown, first, that he himself had to assume a unity of acting and suffering; and second, it can be proved that he does in fact assume it. Thus the first argument falls back on the pure immanent critique that admonishes a lagging behind or even a renunciation of intentions and insists on their fulfillment; while the second argument follows the strategy of the transcending critique, which proceeds immanently only insofar as it takes up the self-transcending aspects of its subject. Within the framework of an essay on the transcending critique, the main emphasis is on the second argument, which is also directly relevant for an understanding of the issue beyond all hermeneutics. Instead, the first gives us a deeper insight into the connection of our problem with the motif that presumably motivated Kierkegaard to take up again in *The Sickness unto Death* the theme already treated in *Either/Or* and to treat it as we have come to know from this book. Its structure in general and in each part is motivated by the intention to demonstrate that no one is able to overcome his despair by himself. After all, the process described in it leads only ever further into despair and not at all out of it.[53] But no one has a salvation from his despair at hand because it itself also transcends the power of human subjects. Thus, the argument operating in the style of a purely immanent critique is: Kierkegaard himself actually had to assume a unity of acting and suffering because he could reach his goal of demonstrating the impossibility of self-redemption only by means of efforts at knowledge which reveal the reason for the impossibility in the condition in need of salvation; it is namely the suffering that limits the scope for action from the start. Or put negatively: the absolute power with which he invests acting contradicts the impotence he presupposes in repudiating ideas of self-salvation.

The contradiction becomes more obvious through a comparison of *The Sickness unto Death* with *Either/Or*. Nowhere does Kierkegaard's concluding analysis of despair diverge so energetically from that of the ethicist in the second volume of his first work as in this point. Based on the assumption that the sickness of despair cannot be cured by even the greatest efforts of the subject, in the 1849 book, Kierkegaard virtually starts a campaign against the therapy the ethicist proposes to the aesthetically living addressee of his letters.[54] After all, the ethicist thinks he can cure the aesthete by advising him to carry the despair he is in to an extreme.[55] The recommendation trusts that a despair carried to its extreme turns into its opposite, into being a self free of despair according to ethical principles. Now, it is true that the ethicist lulls himself into an illusion. But no doubt he has the advantage over his religious critic, the Kierkegaard of 1849, that the practical purpose of his conception is in keeping with its theoretical basis. He knows that despair can be carried to an extreme only through its active appropriation or, as he says, through choice.[56] He interprets this so that the choice only liberates the despair for the act that it was from the beginning.[57] In his view, despair does not first need to be *converted* into action. It is enough to posit it explicitly as an act. The act to be posited is in turn supposed to be identical with despair as such, not merely to form a part of it. Thus, even the ethicist already makes activity absolute.[58] The difference is that by doing that, he acts with completely calculated reason. He has to reduce despair to its active element in order to be able to entrust overcoming it to the activity of the despairing person. The later Kierkegaard, on the other hand, contradicts himself because he holds on to making activity absolute, even though he has given up faith in the ability of the despairing person to cure himself.

However, he also contradicts himself insofar as he uses the denied unity of acting and suffering, this time in a fortunate inconsistency. One of the innovations of the section of despair is, last but not least, the interpretation of despair as an experience of loss.[59] The argumentative turn emerging with that is even more surprising because it refers not only to the despair that Kierkegaard wants to dissolve into semblance, but also to the despair he contrasts with the merely ostensible one as the real despair. Despair over something is presented to us in that section as a loss of the earthly, the despair over oneself as a loss of the eternal. The despair of the eternal, which is identified with the despair over oneself, is more closely defined so that the person afflicted with it has lost the eternal. It does remain the unrivaled truth before which despair over something collapses to semblance even as loss of the earthly. But behind Kierkegaard's back, there is an acknowledgment of the rejected reality, simply because the concept of the loss unites the despair over something and the despair of the eternal. Moreover, as will be shown, all the officially recognized forms of despair are to be subsumed under the despair of the eternal. For despair of the eternal bears and encompasses all manifestations of the sickness that the physician practicing in the 1849 book believes are in his patients. As a result, Kierkegaard virtually defines despair as loss.[60] Thus, his new approach fulfills the conditions that must be given if the unity of acting and suffering is to be justified in its requisite universality.

In the loss of the earthly it can first be seen how every despair is in part constituted by suffering. It is part of the loss of something in the world that it is inflicted on one. It strikes one. It happens even though one naturally does not want it, let alone that one thinks of bringing it about. Thus, if despair is defined by loss, then it cannot only be an act. However, Kierkegaard overshoots the mark when he solidifies the interpretation of despair over something within the horizon of an experience of loss into a definition. Despair over something *is* not loss, it reacts to it; and with this reaction, the act gets a chance, without which it would not be what it is. Kierkegaard's tendency to limit despair to the loss of the earthly corresponds to his suppression of its active meaning. On the other hand, he is absolutely correct in equating despair of the eternal with its loss. For in its case, the loss unites, in itself, the acting and the suffering. It is because of the more complex structure of a loss of the eternal that it is not so easy to understand what that should really mean: to lose the eternal. There is no difficulty understanding what it means to lose a thing in the world. On the other hand, to say that someone loses the eternal does not mean anything sufficiently specific. Aside from the incomprehensibility of the eternal, which will be discussed later, one reason for that is probably the tendency to orient oneself on the model of the loss of the earthly. But the loss of the eternal means primarily that one loses *trust* in it. Thus, it also involves an act. It even seems plausible that this act stands alone, uninflicted. Insofar as it is not actually the eternal that gets lost, but rather trust in it, in other words, a position the subject has taken with regard to the eternal by himself, it may appear as if it was up to the subject to give up his position. But the situation in which a despairing person finds himself must not be described this way. In despair, loss of trust in the eternal means in fact: to lose the eternal itself. The loss of the eternal itself presupposes that the eternal conceals itself from the subject. Just as the eternal evoked trust in it by itself, so it is also based in itself that the subject has no more trust in it. The subject withdraws his trust in the eternal only because the eternal withdraws from him. This may easily be shown by a more precise comparison with the loss of the earthly. Loss of the eternal possesses a richer structure than loss of the earthly in that it comprises the reaction resulting from it. But the act involved in it is none other than the one that reacts. Consequently, it is preceded by a suffering, the suffering of an inaccessible something.

IV

1. If the supernatural loss on the part of suffering is to be made even more plausible, it is necessary to annul the abstraction from the despair of the eternal, which was disregarded by the analysis of the totalizing act. Someone who despairs over some-

thing earthly despairs in truth over the earthly in toto, and whoever despairs over the earthly in toto despairs, in truth, of the eternal.[61] In the same way that despair over something earthly coincides with despair over the earthly in toto, despair of the eternal is in turn identical with both. Here we are not confronted with different cases of despair. Instead, despair over something earthly is also a case of despair over the earthly in toto and ultimately a case of despair of the eternal.[62] Therefore, the three forms would better be described as layers of one and the same phenomenon.[63] This already implies that there is no simple identification, not only because the difference between reflectedness and unreflectedness has a role to play, which is why we are nonetheless dealing with different cases: a person who despairs over something and who has nothing but this something in mind; a person who knows what he is doing when he makes this something into the earthly in toto; and finally, a person who sees through his despair over the earthly in toto as that of the eternal. The three ways of relating to the subject matter of despair also and primarily form one differentiated unity because they are arranged according to the law of the difference of appearance and essence. The despair over something earthly, which is situated on the level of appearance, pertains—in terms of essence—to the earthly in toto, and is—in the deepest depths of its essence—a despair of the eternal. In itself, or fundamentally, it amounts to this despair.

However, despair of the eternal possesses not only a primacy of essence over the despair which appears and which is closer to becoming apparent; it also has a claim to priority in time. Someone who despairs over something earthly and thus over the earthly in toto must already be in despair of the eternal. It seems remarkable that, by contrast, despair over the whole world does not have temporal priority in relation to despair over something in the world. The person despairing over something worldly despairs at once over the totality of the world. He bestows the infinite significance, with which something fills his whole world, on this something only at the very moment it drives him to despair. The special position granted to despair of the eternal in a temporal respect indicates that the main line of demarcation separating essence from its appearance runs between the middle and the lowest level. That is also suggested by the transition to another preposition. While despair over the earthly in toto still shares with despair over something earthly the *over*, the despair of the eternal stands alone with its *of*. The Danish preposition (*om*) corresponds to the German proposition with which we distinguish anxiety about from anxiety of.[64] From the relevance that the change of perspective from the "that in the face of which" (*Wovor*) to the "About-which" (*Worum*) of anxiety has for the knowledge of its essence,[65] it can be estimated how much the insight into the essence of despair depends on the analogous change of perspective. Kierkegaard marks the leap through a different use of the concept of loss. To lose the eternal implies for him more precisely that one *has* lost it.[66] Nowhere in his meditation on the loss of the particular and the earthly in toto does he feel obliged to make such a translation of the present into the perfect. The way he conjugates the concept of loss is practically in line with the finding that despair over something is merely current, while as despair of the eternal it presupposes itself. However, to have lost the eternal implies even more than that the person despairing over something is already in despair of the eternal. Locating the loss in the past also indicates what it means, with regard to the eternal, to suffer a loss. Someone who loses the eternal has already lost it because, even before it becomes an object of a loss, it was a subject of a withdrawal that anticipates the withdrawal of trust for which he is responsible himself. To have lost the eternal means to have *always already* lost it. Its loss was not an act that would be different from the present act of despair merely because it happened in the past. The loss retreats backward behind all acts into a past that cannot be dated.[67]

The idea that despair presupposes itself is a fundamental idea of *The Sickness unto Death*. In the book, it is considered a rule without exception: a person who despairs was already in despair; his current despair simply reveals this.[68] That despair possesses the structure of self-premise seems evident. The idea is one of those that justify the truth claim of the book. But even though it is mentioned long before the change elucidated here,[69] it appeals, at first only anonymously, to the despair of the eternal. Kierkegaard himself would have to confess that. For his demonstration of that structure starts invariably with the despair over something. Thus, in fact, he shows nothing other than what was previously discussed, namely, that despair over something earthly has its logical and temporal *prius* in despair of the eternal. His discussion of the foundational connection between the loss of the earthly and the loss of the eternal can be understood as a belated explanation of the initial guiding idea of a self-premise. But this idea threatens his theory with a danger he clearly does not sense. That is, there is no obstacle to making his insight productive for what he deems authentic despair. In the origin of despair over something out of despair of the eternal, he naturally finds his view confirmed that, taken for itself, the former is mere semblance. Yet there is no plausible reason why the inspection of derivative forms stops with despair over something. Why should the desperation with which someone does or does not will to be himself not also presuppose a despair of the eternal? It was surmised that the desperation of this willing and not willing cannot be—already as desperation—the original desperation, excepting the restrictions of an approach fixated on one's own being. The truly original despair is now revealed as despair of the eternal.

It can be reconstructed quite precisely why Kierkegaard acknowledges only its priority over despair over something, but not its priority vis-à-vis the despair of the self-relation. As briefly mentioned, he identifies it with the despair over oneself.[70] The identification hardly concerns despair over oneself as someone who is such that he cannot be what he planned to be; it refers to the despair over oneself as someone who was so weak as to despair over something. Only in reference to this despair does the identification make some sense. Accordingly, Kierkegaard then goes on to equate despair over oneself explicitly with despair over one's weakness.[71] This despair, however, agrees with the other kind of reflective despair in that it is an indirect one. Kierkegaard himself emphasizes that it represents an advance in comparison with the unreflected despair of weakness. By equating the despair of the eternal with it, he thus reinterprets the provenance of despair over something as its future. He projects what is in back of the despairing person to what lies before and ahead of him. This explains why he cannot perceive the originality of despair of the eternal as absolute and all-encompassing. Nevertheless, the identification of despair of the eternal with despair over one's own weakness makes some sense insofar as the former manifests itself in the latter. In indirect despair, it becomes apparent that direct despair was already rooted in the loss of the eternal.

2. If this is not immediately clear, it is Kierkegaard's conceptualization that is to blame. The thesis that the despairing person could not expand something earthly into the earthly in toto if he did not live in despair of the eternal was judged to merit unconditional approval. However, the approval pertains only to what is meant, not to what is said. With the contrast of the earthly and the eternal, a quasi-Platonic metaphysic creeps into *The Sickness unto Death*.[72] Platonism as such is surely no objection. Metaphysics, which does not have to be quasi-Platonic, need not put up with any reproach, either. On the contrary, it is a testimony to objectivity that the text becomes metaphysical at this point. For a despair that has to be dissected into appearance and essence to be understood *is* a metaphysical phenomenon.[73] Not least therefore does it seem problematic to mark a nihilistic age with the stamp of despair. Men who no longer suffer from the meaningless of everything do not despair for lack of depth. All the more in need of the means of metaphysical

thinking is a phenomenology that inquires what is lacking and thus becomes a critique of its time. But Kierkegaard's phenomenology has a constructivist bent and uses these metaphysical means offensively insofar as it uses them inconsiderately against itself. The contrast of earthly and eternal things collides with his phenomenology's own patterns of interpretation. The concept of eternity contained in this opposition is not only completely unsolved. It is also inconsistent with what is usually designated as eternal in *The Sickness unto Death*. It receives its only definition from its contrast to the concept of the earthly. Yet everything else that is otherwise called eternal in our text excludes such a contrast.

Except for the two meanings in question here, the concept of the eternal gives no information in our text about their relation to one another and with regard to the meaning in question. The concept means either the eternal, which, as an element in the synthesis to be established in the consummation of human Dasein, is harnessed together with the element of temporality,[74] or an element that Kierkegaard attributes to the self. This is ambiguous even in itself: it is sometimes called an eternal element in the self and sometimes one in the person, which is to be identical with the self.[75] The element of synthesis is the element most easily to be thought of as opposed to the earthly, particularly since the earthly in *The Sickness unto Death* replaces the temporal. After all, it stands opposite the temporal. But the establishment of the synthesis annuls, precisely, the metaphysical opposition. Classifying the eternal, which is to be united with its other, as a possibility shifts it into a future in which it can fall only insofar as we have to make a decision for eternity in time. The being-in-time of the decision temporalizes even eternity which, as a future one itself, is already temporal in itself. What is eternal in the self, or the self as what is eternal in man, does not even obey the oppositional schema in terms of its approach. If we stick to the version that asserts an identity between the eternal and the self, then it seems reasonable to interpret the concept that requires clarification as a temporalized expression for the absolute to which Kierkegaard elevates the baseless process of relating oneself to oneself. But the absolute comprises overcoming an opposition that constrains the eternal by way of the earthly. The other variant is too vague for us to be able to show it in this opposition. If, however, we examine what are, essentially, the three meanings of the concept of eternity with regard to the question of whether the conception of a despair of the eternal takes up one of them and, if so, which one, then the only remaining candidate to be taken seriously is the eternal in the self. It is just as impossible to despair of the eternal that is one with the self as it is impossible to despair of the eternal that is incorporated within our being human, at least if, in the loss suffered, something other withdraws itself. Under this condition, the eternal in the self, if taken at face value, naturally has no chance at all of passing the test. After all, the suggested immanence does not in the least tolerate something other. The eternal in the self is a possible link only if we may assume that *The Sickness unto Death* locks it into the self because it mystifies it. But for its demystification, it is not enough to burst the shell. First of all, the concept of the eternal itself must be destroyed and what is hidden behind it exposed.[76]

In the so-called despair of the eternal, the person despairs of *that which saves*. From that, it becomes plausible that and how it manifests itself in his despair over his weakness. If someone despairs not only *in* weakness, but also *over* it, this is because he has lost his trust in what saves him as that which would be able to redeem him from his weakness. Substituting the eternal with that which saves involves the same thing as the other operations of a transcending critique: it also extends only the line, as it were, on which the criticized theory transcends itself. The connection between the most primordial despair and that advanced despair is already an example of that. Wrong as it is to compound the two, it nevertheless reveals an idea that the eternal must be decoded as a cipher for that which saves. *The Sick-*

ness unto Death provides an even more direct preliminary work for its deciphering. When Kierkegaard describes the person despairing of the eternal as someone who does not want to be comforted and healed by the eternal,[77] he basically carries out the translation himself. He comes even closer to grasping what saves us when he observes that we despair of that which releases us from despair.[78] However, the ensuing collection of possible subject matters of a "despair of" also makes the reader aware of the limit the self-transcending theory apparently cannot break through. On the one hand, that which saves—under the name of salvation—becomes a direct subject matter. On the other hand, it loses its profile by being enumerated as one subject matter among others. The outlines become blurred not so much because it appears together with other things that have nothing saving about them, but rather because of the curious circumstance that, on the contrary, what is saving about the ostensibly different other subject matters remains unobserved. Thus, Kierkegaard, who tacks one's own strength onto salvation, seems not to notice that we could hardly despair of our own strength as he comprehends it if it were not also more than something that is our own, that is the basis of all our activity, as which it promises us salvation. How dull is Kierkegaard's view of saving is revealed primarily by the fact that he tacks salvation onto the eternal as if it were not yet contained in it. The fact puts it on record: even though he sees what saves us, what eludes him is that what he sees there is the eternal. More precisely, he does not identify that which saves as the all-encompassing principle, which, in his hands, becomes the eternal.

If he had recognized the general "of which" of despair in that, he would not have unwittingly made a serious error. In his view, we always know over what we despair, but usually not of what we despair.[79] In reality, we also know this. Our knowledge results from the fact that what we despair of, no matter its nature in a concrete case, fundamentally and in general is that which saves. Even if in certain situations, we cannot imagine anything specific by that, unconsciousness of what saves us as such is absolutely out of the question. What it would amount to is that we would not be in despair at all. For despair in itself is not only a loss of that which saves; as an act, it also presupposes an awareness of what gets lost in it. In turn, Kierkegaard's negation of our knowledge follows from his covering up of what saves us. He projects the unconsciousness of his way of dealing with the concept of eternity onto those persons to whom he offers this concept as a means of understanding their despair. People do not know what they despair of only insofar as they do not know what to do with the eternal, while they are assured that they despair of it.

3. We must bring into slightly sharper focus the limits the theory encounters in the process of transcending itself. Ultimately, Kierkegaard covers up that to despair *as such* means to despair of that which saves. But by doing that, he denies his own conception. The fact that despair is fundamentally and wholly a despair of that which saves seems at first to be merely a consequence of our considerations here. To be sure, if it is correct that the so-called despair of the eternal underlies every despair, then this is also correct: every despair can be traced back to the despair that the so-called despair of the eternal aims at, which is the despair of that which saves. However, it is the despair portrayed in *The Sickness unto Death* itself which in all its forms is based on the despair of that which saves. This can be inferred conclusively from its opposition to faith. Kierkegaard may have various concepts of faith even in his book of 1849. But one of them seems geared especially to the goal of his book. According to this concept, to believe means to have trust that everything is possible.[80] Correspondingly, to despair means to lose and have lost the trust that everything is possible. Now Kierkegaard regards possibility as the one thing that saves.[81] Thus, he himself is pressed to understand despair as such as originating from a loss of what saves us. That he does indeed understand it as

originating from that is shown especially by his description of the path taken by the constantly intensifying despair. The path ends, as a wrong path, in the demonic. In it, defiance, which has already intensified from arrogance to rebellion, undergoes another intensification. The most extreme defiance—the defiance of despair becoming demonic—consists in the fact that one does not want to let himself be saved.[82] But not to let oneself be saved can be the most extreme of despair only because, from the very beginning, this was of a loss of what saves us.

The concept of a faith that trusts that everything is possible develops, first of all, the precise meaning of the substitution of the eternal with that which saves. It aims at the genuine faith in Jesus, the faith Jesus himself had, the model of faith *in* Jesus as Christ.[83] But from the biblical and thus orthodox concept of faith, Kierkegaard develops a completely unorthodox idea of God. He already distances himself from orthodoxy with a risky radicalization. He sharpens the promise of the New Testament, that nothing is impossible with God and for God, into the thesis that God *is* this fact, that everything is possible. But the distance becomes a separation with the reversal of the proposition: That everything is possible, that is God.[84] Of course, Kierkegaard does not want the reversed proposition to be understood as it sounds in the mouths of the reductionist theoreticians of his time. He is far from asserting that what we incorrectly call God is in reality nothing but the infinite space of possibility. Rather, he wants to convince us that God is manifested whenever our possibilities become unlimited. Instead of dissolving God into unlimited possibility, he ascribes unlimited possibility to God. But unlimited possibility or the fact that even the impossible becomes possible is what saves us. Thus, Kierkegaard's conclusion is: in everything that saves us, God is present. His conclusion is no doubt based on the premise that in the end, only God Himself can save. But because of this he traces any salvation that is not immediately a work of God back to God. Ultimately, the argument goes, if God alone is what saves us, then God is in everything that saves us. At least the conclusion also contains the other, somewhat opposite premise, that a temporary salvation can come from something other than God. For example, one's own strength could save. It would especially be a salvation if one's fellow man would commit himself to the person in despair.[85] The popular proposal of replacing the completely Other with the other person, with the psychoanalyst, if need be, dismantles the theory not only by withdrawing its theological ground. It also destroys it, even more so, by restoring an alternative which circumvents the theory altogether.

Kierkegaard's unorthodox idea of God relates that which saves with the eternal, as the substitute of which it was introduced. There is, of course, no identity of meaning between the concept to be substituted and its substitute. That which saves as such has hardly anything to do with the eternal. It takes on the meaning of an eternal only as a result of its grounding in a God who alone is able to save absolutely. Thus, if we do not want to do without the eternal altogether in its substitution by that which saves, we must be careful not to eliminate God from the theory, following, for example, the above proposal; on the contrary, we must anchor Him even deeper in the foundation of the theory. The destruction of metaphysics in the thought of an eternal, which opposes the earthly, does not do away with theology at all; it makes room for theology. If *The Sickness unto Death* is purified of its quasi-Platonic two-world doctrine, which is an alien body in it, the eternal, which Kierkegaard (as a Platonist in this respect, too) accommodates *in* the self, is revealed as the power that has established the self, as the God *through* which the self is what it is.[86] On its own ground, the eternal is the eternity of God and, as the subject matter of faith, that which saves not just temporarily but forever. The faith that trusts that everything is possible is only ostensibly excluded from the definition claiming that to have faith is to be grounded transparently in the power that has established the self. The fact that this definition in our case is used right at the very beginning and quite explicitly at the end of the book[87] seems to confirm that *it* merits the privilege which was ascribed to the concept of faith as having trust in that which saves, namely, to be the concept of faith especially characteristic of *The Sickness unto Death*. In truth, the definition cannot deny the status of this concept, since it essentially captures the same thing. To rest transparently in God means, precisely, to trust that everything is possible. The concept of faith as grounding oneself in God is more comprehensive only insofar as it takes into account that the self reflects the synthetically composed being human in its entirety, not only the element of possibility, but also that of necessity. The possibility that makes up one pole of the synthesis appears on the level of the self in the form of infinitely relating oneself to oneself, the necessity on the other pole appears as the facticity of being established.[88] The three meanings of the concept of eternity claimed unsystematically in *The Sickness unto Death* are connected so that the eternal as that which saves forever extends, even in the existentiell sense, the possibility that is to be ascribed to the eternal as an element of the synthesis, the possibility which is structurally unlimited in the eternal that is identical with the self. But by realizing this unlimitation, someone who in faith grounds himself in God submits to the limit established in the establishment of his self. The genuine concept of faith of our text is conceived so that it in turn reflects back, in the self, the reflection of the synthesis. Its two-sidedness corresponds exactly to the two sides of the self. That the study of Kierkegaard's fundamental principle has defined this concept only in terms of one side, that of self-humiliation, is because of its immanence. The other side, being set free for the insight that everything is possible, is revealed only by a transcending perspective which perceives a trust whose relation to God goes beyond the reflective one. But trust in the all-enabling God is actually so much a part of faith that it is to be conceived as part of the self-humiliation. Humility can ward off the appearance of heteronomy only if it is thought of as being part of that trust. The ambiguous self-humiliation before God that is implied by a self-acceptance in one's pre-given Dasein would become a heteronomous self-acceptance[89] if the darkness of facticity were not illuminated by the freedom promised by the thought: God is this that everything is possible, and that everything is possible, that is God.[90]

As we said, the God on which Kierkegaard's theory of despair is constructed must be anchored even more deeply in the theory if the substitution of the eternal by that which saves does not amount to abandoning that God. The theological basis of the theory is secured precisely by recognizing God even in the eternal which appears as the earthly's other within the horizon of a quasi-Platonic metaphysic. To be sure, the if clause does make such a deepening and extension of the idea of God dependent on a condition that does not have to be strictly fulfilled in any case. A person who conceives the eternal as that which saves no longer needs to think of that which saves as the eternal. Reducing the eternal to that which saves would not be a substitution if it were subject to the need to save even the eternal itself.

Nonetheless, the talk of an eternal that promises salvation acquires a kind of functional necessity within the framework of Kierkegaard's theory. It is hard to see that the concept of despair, as conceived in *The Sickness unto Death*, once served, in *Either/Or*, as a means to interpret nihilism. This function appears only in those places where the theory transcends itself. That Kierkegaard secretly continued his debate with nihilism is first revealed where he inserts the figure of loss in his field of inquiry. At the same moment, he takes up the ostensibly interrupted contact with nihilistic experiences of loss. The contact is already established by the loss of the earthly. The heuristic strength of the guiding concept passes its first serious test as soon as it turns out that despair makes *the* earthly out of earthly things. For it thus invalidates everything in the world. But Kierkegaard has always correctly distinguished nihilism from a merely pessimistic world-view for which, as in the eyes of Ecclesiastes, there is nothing *new under the sun*. The experience of being becomes nihilistic only in transcending the earthly. Thus, the concept of despair proves its conclusive value as an interpretive category for nihilism only with the demonstration that in the loss of the earthly the eternal gets lost. In fact, to make full use of its interpretive strength, it is necessary to understand and pronounce the eternal *as* eternal. Even its opposition to the earthly acquires a certain validity in the service of the interpretation of nihilism, namely as one that, in keeping with the relation of nihilism and metaphysics, is sublated. Yes, now it becomes clear that by the loss of what saves, we must understand something very comprehensive if it is to be useful for an appropriate description of nihilistic experiences of loss. It must include the loss of meaning. That which saves is itself to be grasped as that which gives meaning. The concept of the eternal already reaches out into the dimension of meaning by itself, as it were, insofar as it aims in its Platonic meaning at a being that, since it is permanent, can be relied on and satisfies the need for security. As a cipher for the living source of all meaning, however, we can read it only if we remove it from the context of metaphysics and apply it to God. Despair—that is also the loss of confidence in a God Who could save us through His vitality forever from the destitution of a life emptied of meaning.

V

1. Kierkegaard interprets faith as trust that everything is possible in the section that deals with the despair of necessity, that is the despair in which what the person lacks is possibility. The believing person reacts to the "nothing is possible" of the person in such despair with the assertion that everything is possible. Here what Kierkegaard repeats incessantly is more than plain: that faith presupposes despair. The leap into the abyss of the idea that everything is possible for God appears as the only

way out of a situation in which nothing is possible for the person anymore. This correlation stands out even more clearly against the background of the complementary despair, which, as a despair of possibility, is based on a lack of necessity. Someone who lives in such despair thinks and acts according to the principle: everything is possible.[91] But the "everything is possible" of belief is different from the "everything is possible" of the unlimiting despair because it has gone through the "nothing is possible" of limiting despair. It is unequivocally understood as God's cause only if it is clear that the person himself has no more possibility.[92] Therefore, faith puts itself into an opposition with both forms of despair. It leaves the despair of possibility behind by acknowledging the limitation established in the establishment of the self; and it sets itself apart from the despair of necessity by finding consolation in the idea of a God for Whom everything is possible. Consequently, reversing the real course of things in his account, Kierkegaard defines both forms of despair by the negation of the corresponding movements of faith: a person who is entirely wrapped up in possibility does not submit to the necessity in the self,[93] and a person who is drowned in necessity is not open to the possibility in God. Thus, Kierkegaard depicts the two sides of faith onto the two forms of despair. It is important to realize the consequences of that for despair. Since faith has no more than the two sides of self-humiliation before God and depending on God, the distinction between modalities of a despairing lack of faith must also be regarded as a complete disjunction. People surrender to disbelief either through the illusionary view that everything is possible for them or through their fixation on the fact that nothing is possible for them.

Kierkegaard's procedure in the whole text, which concludes with the considerations on the despair of possibility and the despair of necessity, suits this finding. A first glance is enough to show that the attempt undertaken here, to get closer to the goal of making the preliminary projection concrete by way of reflecting on the elements of the synthesis, is carried out only very fragmentarily. From the beginning, Kierkegaard refrains from deriving despair from the failure of that synthesis, whose elements are the temporal and the eternal.[94] The sections oriented to the synthesis of possibility and necessity are preceded merely by those that explain the phenomenon by making infinitude or finitude absolute. But the reduction of the program is essentially more far-reaching. That is, in these sections despair practically does not appear. The transcending critique seeks to demonstrate not only that Kierkegaard excludes a great deal from his field of inquiry, what in truth is part of his subject; it is also to prove that he includes a great deal that is in fact alien to his subject. As we have seen, both result from his identification of despair with the deficiency of relating oneself to oneself. He does not discuss any despair that lies beyond this deficiency; and he also discusses such a deficiency which in truth is not despair. The sections on the polar unilateralist reductions of infinitude and finitude in *The Sickness unto Death* are the main retreats for a self-relation that is not in despair at all, even if it is deficient. Contrary to the intention of the author who presents everything formulated in those sections as despair because he considers everyone in despair who does not become himself by holding together the poles of his being human, these sections teach precisely how one can go through life without even feeling a sense of lack.[95] Such a feeling of well-being, which does not accord well with true despair, stands out not only from the depression of one who gets lost in necessity; it also contrasts thoroughly with the excess of one who disappears in possibility.[96] For making possibility absolute presupposes an act to be renewed incessantly, which severs possibility from its actualization, and ridding it of actuality generates a feeling of emptiness that can be called despaired. But from all that, we must draw the conclusion: the synthetic-theoretical view may consider only the despair of possibility and of necessity as real despair.[97]

This recognition is to be linked with the insight we gained in the analysis of the relation to faith of both forms of despair.

The link requires two more corrections of Kierkegaard's self-conception. First: behind the façade of a structure housing allegedly calm forms, a process is taking place. The process starts with despair of possibility, then forces this into despair of necessity and finally breaks off with the leap into faith. Second: the despair considered in the synthetic theory changes from an active to a predominantly passive despair. In both respects, the difference between this despair and the despair examined in terms of consciousness loses its sharp distinction. The movement from acting to being acted on also parallels the path that is ultimately pursued by the despair constantly increasing in consciousness and thus admittedly advancing.[98] In it, what takes place only underground comes to light. With the admission that nothing is possible any more, despair professes the weakness that returns covertly on the height of defiance. The suffering that Kierkegaard disregards by immediately moving on to the defiance reacting to it is discussed here in its own desperation.

However, someone who gets drowned in necessity suffers differently from someone who rebels in defiance. To be sure, their respective suffering does have something in common, insofar as the latter's enjoyment of experimentation is ruined by the pain he discovers in his pre-given existence, and as the former's joy in life is lost in the possibility that is rid of actuality because he gets into a situation in which nothing is possible anymore. But while the suffering that is compensated for by defiance is a pure suffering, the suffering that is caused by an aporetic situation contains an element of activity. The person who is overcome by despair of necessity realizes himself that nothing is possible anymore. The purity of suffering processed in defiance attests only to its exclusion from the despair that Kierkegaard places only in defiance itself. Correspondingly, the impurity of suffering that causes the eclipse of the horizon of possibility documents his desperation. For the act taken up in it is the totalizing act of despair—in the form of a negative totalization. If the despair of possibility progresses from the part to the whole by spreading the appearance as if anything were possible, so the despair of necessity takes the same step with a negation that destroys the appearance so thoroughly that nothing remains of possibility. The collaboration of activity, however, does not mean that the suffering is diminished. Its intensity exceeds even the suffering that is covered up by defiance. On the one hand, it is also totalized in itself. The person who runs off into defiance suffers, for one minuscule moment, from something particular, while the person choked with necessity already has the whole before him as a suffering person. On the other hand, his suffering wrenches him beyond himself. Even though the particular on which the experiment with oneself founders is also something pre-given, it is nonetheless part of one's own Dasein. However, the whole that plunges one into the despair of necessity is, already as a source of suffering, the whole of the world. If the nihilism that usually appears merely in the background of the picture presses to the foreground anywhere in *The Sickness unto Death*, it is at the last stage of the course through the deficiencies of the self-relation. It is nowhere as conspicuous as here that, as a nihilistic experience, despair registers an objective condition of the whole world. It emerges in a situation that is itself in despair, as it were. The thesis that faith presupposes it can be interpreted in terms of the philosophy of history by making it concrete with the statement that Kierkegaard's special faith in an all-enabling God had its hour only in the night of the world that constricts the activity of humans before all subjective arbitrariness to the acknowledgment of the fact that nothing is possible for them anymore.

A mediation between acting and suffering that assimilates suffering to the self-activity of the accountable subject without making it lose the priority it merits as a suffering of reality, casts a sharper light on the process in which the act changes into a suffering mediated in such a way. Inasmuch as life in the possibility devoid of reality, aside from its accompanying feeling of emptiness, has no element of suffering, it does not yet seem to be in despair in the full sense of the word, but rather on an antecedent stage prior to despair.[99] In contrast, despair par excellence rises from the abyss of a universalized despair.[100] Another index for a development from seed to blossom is the differentiated way Kierkegaard unfolds the opposing failures of the synthesis against the contrasting foil of faith. Indeed, as we said, he defines both through a negation of their respective acts of faith. But while in the so-called despair of possibility he merely negates what characterizes a faith that remains anonymous, he puts the despair of necessity into a negative relation to a faith called by its name. It is in constant opposition to this despair that he develops his *concept* of faith. He can seize the opportunity for that only because he keeps dwelling on an exemplary despair. The distinction that is allotted the despair of necessity because Kierkegaard selects this despair, and only it, as the place for his discussion of faith is meant for the despair that is distinguished by itself.

Now, the despair of necessity is in fact hopelessness. A person who despairs in view of the fact that nothing is possible pursues a negative totalization by letting all hope go. But *desperatio* does not merely get a place in the framework of the theory that sought to understand a despair that is understood literally, derived from a totalization of doubt, other than as abandonment of hope. If only this were the case, the self-conception of this theory would remain intact. Kierkegaard gladly concedes that it is also a form of despair not to hope for the removal of an earthly need.[101] But it is precisely the tone in which Kierkegaard says such things that reveals how certain it seems to him that despair initially, before its diversification into special manifestations, is not an abandonment of hope. It is only on the basis of this preconception that he can find the desperation of a lack of hope remarkable at all. However, judging by Kierkegaard's own criteria, if the despair of necessity is the despair par excellence, then the hopelessness it amounts to seems to take the place of what was projected as an alternative to it. Then it seems as if the return of *desperatio* has to be interpreted so that on its return, its successor resigns. It looks as if the theory that intended a paradigm shift is ultimately forced to give back control to the usurped paradigm.

The same impression may be gained from the other side, from the perspective on the fate suffered by the despair that totalizes doubt. For the curious light-heartedness with which the people observed by Kierkegaard live beyond synthesizing finitude and infinitude provokes the question of whether they are spared an instinctively realized despair possibly because they are far from totalizing a doubt. From the point of view of the synthesis, a despair emerging from a totalization of doubt would be represented so that people would stagger back and forth between a fixation on finitude and a fixation on infinitude. Only in such staggering would their oscillation, which as in doubt is restricted to an intellectual act, become a movement shattering their whole existence.[102] It alone would be the existential rupture, as which the despair, taken literally, outdoes doubt. But we find no trace of such staggering in the text that examines the issue under the aspect of the synthesis. The mutually exclusive followers of finitude and infinitude feel so good about themselves because they settle down in their corner and arrange themselves comfortably. Inasmuch as Kierkegaard denies the process that liquefies at least the final forms behind his back, he does not even allow them to get up now and then and start moving. Thus he still blocks up the only hole through which the staggering could enter his structure and disturb the peace of its inhabitants. In this way, he locks out the very despair for which he erected the structure, the despair that totalizes doubt. As far as the synthetic-theoretical theory does examine real despair, this is due to the reversal that brings *desperatio* into control.

2. To get a better understanding of what is going on here, we have to realize what Kierkegaard really had in mind when he projected a concept of despair oriented to the totalization of doubt, in which hopelessness is reduced to an element. Since a

despair that turns the subject against himself bears the stamp of modernity, what is new in it should become especially clear against the background of a premodern conception. Kierkegaard approached his project of a history of freedom early on, and the way this history demonstrates the genesis of freedom in the sequence of anxiety, melancholy, and despair is indebted to the tradition stretching from the first Christian centuries to the late Middle Ages, which contrasts spiritual joy to the *acedia*, the sloth of the heart. Kierkegaard, who mentions *acedia* explicitly in his considerations of melancholy, was probably also aware that the designated mixture of surfeit and inner emptiness was regarded as the source of despair. Even Thomas Aquinas, the heir of this thousand-year-old tradition, traced *desperatio* back to *acedia*.[103] Presumably, this was equally familiar to the former student of theology. The context in which the reduction to Thomas Aquinas is embedded anticipates so much of *The Sickness unto Death* that its independence from Aquinas hardly seems credible. Thomas Aquinas especially prepares the interpretation of despair as sin.[104] In his view, *desperatio* is one of the vices in which theological virtues get lost.[105] Since the theological virtues are the greatest, Thomas even counts the abandonment of hope as the greatest sin.[106] It is inherent in his differentiation of *desperatio* from *odium Dei* and from *infidelitas* that he cannot yet identify it with sin per se, and thus he cannot yet reverse the proposition that maintains that despair is sin, either. However, he does already know of a despair in which sin becomes reflective as it were: the *desperatio* that grows out of the horror over one's own sin[107] points forward to the sin of despairing over one's sin. Moreover, precisely through the contrast with *infidelitas*, Aquinas is attentive to a feature that advances to being the dominating one in Kierkegaard: despair is not a matter of the intellect, it falls in the sphere of the will.[108]

It would be tempting to retell the essential genesis of freedom from a historical perspective and to register the old doctrine of the origin of *desperatio* from *acedia* in Kierkegaard's concept of despair. For in the breakthrough of despair from a mood overcoming and depressing men from outside, it can be illustrated with examples that *The Sickness unto Death* had to position the weakness of suffering deeper than it actually does. To be sure, *acedia* would be sufficiently visible in its dark-toned proper colors only against the foil of the melancholy of antiquity, the *acedia* against which Renaissance melancholy rose.[109] It has nothing of all that lightens black bile, nothing of the transcending impetus that makes melancholy the sickness of the outstanding person and which inspires that person intellectually. Here, another aspect of the Medieval conception is to be envisaged, the one that Kierkegaard will fundamentally change.

Naturally, there are great divides cutting through the common ground of the theology of sin. By contrasting despair with hope, Aquinas excludes the opportunity seized by Kierkegaard to put despair into an opposition to faith. In his view, it is not only different from disbelief but conceivable without it.[110] Insofar as it was probably this change of opposing despair to faith that caused Kierkegaard to approach it from the point of view of doubt, this dissent must not be underestimated. But *desperatio* receives its specific imprint in Aquinas only because he also develops a contrast in the way in which the contrast with hope can be defined. Following the model of the Aristotelian doctrine of virtues, he also situates the theological virtue in the middle between two extremes. Thus, the right measure that is established for us through the command to hope is missed not only by the person who has let all hope go; the person who succumbs to an excessive hope misses it, too. *Desperatio* confronts a *praesumptio* in which hope turns into its opposite through hypertrophy.[111] The construction is an exemplary demonstration of the mediation so characteristic of the High Middle Ages, between Antiquity and Christianity. On the one hand, it recalls the skepticism of Antiquity vis-à-vis a human existence torn between too little and too much hope. On the other, it totalizes the deficit and the excess in Christian spirit into negations of hope. If the negative pole is occupied by a hopelessness that would have been hard for the Greeks to imagine, the ostensibly positive pole has a self-confidence that, in its own way, opposes the hope that always has its share of uncertainty. A *praesumptio* in itself is nothing but a presupposition. Husserl talks of the presumptive style of consciousness, protentional in its intentionality, constantly rushing ahead through presuppositions. Yet the presumption becomes sinful when the subject makes it on his own, when it thinks it is so certain of its future that it relies entirely on itself. Thomas Aquinas distinguishes two kinds of *praesumptio*, a first kind in which the subject relies on its own strength, even if it is overtaxed; and a second kind, in which it relies on the mercy or power of God, without undertaking the efforts through which it would have to prove itself worthy of divine assistance. The first kind rises from vanity (*inanis gloria*), the second from that arrogance (*superbia*) into which Christian thinking transforms the ancient hubris, the presumptuousness of a bottomless pride.[112]

3. Kierkegaard goes beyond Aquinas primarily by expanding the concept of despair, which was restricted to *desperatio*, to *praesumptio*. Seen against the background of the Medieval conception, the innovation of his projection is that he discovers an independent form of despair in *praesumptio*. That he even elevates this form to the level of an original and final form can be explained by the exuberance of his joy of discovery. Indeed, a *praesumptio* identified as despair can no longer be the one that Aquinas thought of. Kierkegaard disconnects it from its opposition to faith. But he also uncouples that form of despair from the contrast with hope which in Aquinas appears in the role of *desperatio*, precisely as despair in opposition to *spes*. The transformation of both forms is in turn contingent on the fact that initially the comprehensive despair itself demands a transformation corresponding to its changed position. Stretched between the extremes that Aquinas confronts as *desperatio* and

praesumptio, it must become what its German name refers to: a rupture. The effects of this change on the understanding of both forms can be seen especially well in the text about the failures of the synthesis. Here, Kierkegaard combines finitude and necessity in the limited, infinitude and possibility in the unlimited. He seems to cite the oldest opposition, of *peras* and *apeiron*,[113] to explain that despair intensifies into the utmost extreme. In return, in the complementary text on willing and not willing to be oneself, the origin of the forms can be seen more clearly. The despair in weakness succeeds *desperatio*, the despair of defiance is heir to *praesumptio*. It is not accidental that Kierkegaard also sees pride on the side of the latter.[114] The provenance becomes strikingly obvious as soon as we realize that the opposite of weakness is really strength. Beneath defiance, the strength the presumptuous person thinks he is capable of can be seen. We can even still pursue the path on which strength has taken on the appearance of defiance. To include *praesumptio* in despair and even seeking its main focus in it was clearly inspired by Goethe's *Faust*.[115] The model for the portrait of *praesumptio* seems to have been not so much Faust himself as Mephistopheles. In any case, with the term "defiance," Kierkegaard characterizes the devil's despair the first time he uses it in *The Sickness unto Death*.[116] This may be a clue that it was the figure of Mephistopheles that prompted him especially to rechristen the arrogance based on a feeling of strength as "defiance." More precisely, his orientation to it is partly to blame that, along with the rebellious attitude of one who wills to be himself for the sake of disavowing God, he also forces the high-handedness of the person constructing himself under the concept of defiance. The concept of defiance in itself is only fit to mark the revolt, and only revolt has its model in the rebellion of the Fallen Angel. However, the arrogant self-construction would have been discussed more appropriately if it had kept its old name and had not identified itself verbally as *praesumptio*. The mentality behind it is actually not defiance but *superbia*, the pride of one who dares to project himself in abstraction from his divinely established facticity. Therefore, we must bear in mind that it was the arrogance of constructivist self-projection that Kierkegaard confronts with the impotence of defeatist self-rejection in the pivotal approach of his general theory. Thus, it is in despair to will to be oneself that administers, initially and primarily, the legacy of *praesumptio*.

Now, if the secret process that Kierkegaard pursues in his description of correlative ways of failing the formation of a synthesis amounts to hopelessness, then the despair of defiance cannot remain unaffected by that. Just as the despair of necessity revealed as hopelessness itself corresponds structurally to the despair in weakness, so there is also a structural equivalence between the despair of possibility and the despair of defiance. A person who leaps from possibility to possibility without actualizing anything usually forms even a personal union with the person who in his self-projection leaps over his pre-given existence. The fact that that process begins as a real process of despair only with ridding possibility of actuality makes the proportional analogy even more obvious: true despair can be only the despair of possibility or the despair of necessity, because in their realm there is nothing but defiance or weakness.[117] The fate of despair considered in terms of the synthetic theory affects that of defiance first by questioning its privileging. If the despair of necessity is despair par excellence and the despair of possibility, strictly speaking, is merely a preliminary stage prior to it, then the sequence of weakness and defiance understood as an order of rank has to be reversed: the despair lurking in defiance breaks out unbridled in weakness. In this respect, the result attained by the critical analysis of the course of the synthetic-theoretical inquiry only confirms the findings attained by comprehending the course of the inquiry in terms of the theory of consciousness. But inasmuch as the despair considered in terms of the synthetic-theoretical view leads to hopelessness, its fate affects defiance, second, because the *praesumptio* preserved in it sinks back into *desperatio*; and thus we gain a new insight with regard to the previous discoveries. The sinking back of *praesumptio* into *desperatio* is more than a victory of one form over the other. In that process, the whole concept of despair that guided the interpretation of *praesumptio* as a form of despair becomes shaky. This form, which once was regarded as the despair per se regains its original validity by gaining control of the form it replaced, and this happens at the expense of the fundamental understanding of despair that instigated the removal.

However, it is not as it seemed to be before the digression on Thomas Aquinas: that the despair conceived in terms of loss of hope displaced completely the despair constructed in terms of the model of rupture. The comparison of the two conceptions also shows what it is that Aquinas cannot register and that enters only into Kierkegaard's model. Only Kierkegaard can elucidate a desperation that differs qualitatively from mere despondency, the desperation of an act that no one would think of calling despondent. But the concept of despair derived from the literal meaning of the word *fortvivelse* can no longer be linked with the claim that it represents an alternative to *desperatio*. Indeed, in the Danish word, an experience finds expression that is different from the experience sedimented in the Latin word, and because it is part of a later age, it may also be more advanced. But it also shows good sense that the Anglo-Saxon and Romance languages did not tear out the older root. In the discourse on the issue, there is no special Germanic way. The issue has taken up nonsimultaneous experiences which a general understanding must nevertheless comprehend simultaneously. The claim that a concept of despair describing the figure of a totalization of doubt puts *desperatio* on a deeper foundation cannot be maintained, either. Rather, the concept oriented to an abandonment of hope seems to afford, for its part, a foundation on which the ostensibly alternative concept is to be applied.[118]

4. *The Sickness unto Death* says at one point that Mephistopheles is right when he declares that nothing is more miserable than a devil who despairs.[119] Remarkably, Kierkegaard does not

explain to us why he can applaud this declaration even though he accuses the devil of a despair that ranks for him in the highest place, the most unconditional defiance. In truth, his approval reveals the thoroughly questionable nature of the project of claiming *praesumptio* for a despair that surpasses presumptuous pride with a diabolically rebellious defiance. Self-problematization can also be turned into a positive matter and taken as a transcending of one's self, in which the truth wins out against a theory that tends to suppress it. Kierkegaard's theory of despair transcends itself one last time by retreating, of its own accord, to the deeper foundation that is attributed to it at first glance from outside by the conception of despair as hopelessness. In view of its movement pursued here, it may even be asserted: it *has* already retreated to it. It took the step backward by grounding all despair in the despair of the eternal. To despair of the eternal—in the critique starting with the self-transcending elements of the theory—means to lose trust in that which saves us. But what still appears in the Kierkegaardian perspective of faith as loss of trust is revealed from the older reference point of despair as an abandonment of hope.

All we need to do now is to explore how the *desperatio*, which Kierkegaard himself in fact thrusts into the very center of his theory, relates to its theory-external original prototype. However, for that, a transcending critique is again necessary. Although Kierkegaard emphasizes temporality in human Dasein, not only out of consideration for its composition from the temporal and the eternal, but also by interpreting it as a synthesis of finitude and infinitude, necessity and possibility, and even though he hangs the structure of his theory of despair in the scaffolding of his continuously temporalized anthropology, at least where he examines despair under the aspect of the failure of the synthesis,[120] he really is not investigating despair in terms of its time structure. This is even more remarkable because he does describe the earlier stages of the history of freedom in terms of a theory of time. It is above all anxiety that he examines in terms of its temporal condition. There are indeed also comments in *The Sickness unto Death* such as that the youth despairs over the future, the adult over the past.[121] But such comments only make the lack more critical. They illustrate how much Kierkegaard pushes the temporality of despair away into the empirical realm when, in fact, it is precisely in the temporal implications of his approach that there is a potential to be exploited. Once this potential is revealed, it is instantly clear that Kierkegaard not only adopts the *desperatio*, but rather develops it further and does so according to *its* rules, definitely not in the direction of the goal he pursues in departing from it.

Aquinas conceives of *desperare de* as a despairing of. That follows unequivocally from the theological context. A despair that opposes a hope aimed at God can be thought of only as despair *of* this God. Aquinas sees it mainly as a despair of God's mercy. That by *de* he understands *of* can be seen just as clearly in his secular examples. The physician with whom he demonstrates his concept does not despair over the inability to cure a patient; he despairs over his curing.[122] Thus, the *desperatio* refers to the future just as the *praesumptio* does, whose reference to the future is indicated unmistakably by the language used. Weakness and defiance in Kierkegaard are joint heirs of futurity. More precisely: weakness inherits it insofar as it manifests itself in the direct not willing to be oneself, and defiance inherits it insofar as it makes its presence felt in the indirectly not willing to be oneself, that is, in willing to be what one is not. By going far beyond the *praesumptio* with the advance to rebellious defiance, Kierkegaard also leaves behind the level of comparable temporal relations. But the defiance of in despair to will to be oneself, which remains under the spell of not willing to be oneself, reflects the kind of "living ahead" invested in it. That defiance is the presumptuousness of the person constructing himself, who believes he can master the future by breaking free from everything that is pre-given. By contrast, that weakness appears in the temporal framework as the despondency of the person who shies away from taking his future in his own hands.

Kierkegaard turns away from the future only when he focuses on the despair over something. Then he turns to the past. For just as despair of is essentially oriented to the future, so despair over is essentially defined by the past. We can despair over only something that has already happened. Despair over is the same as despair of in the sense that it has its basis in despair of. Consequently, the despair explained in this way extends into the future as well as the past. What Kierkegaard divides into different ages belongs together in its essential structure. When it was previously asserted that Kierkegaard did not examine despair in terms of its temporal structure, what was meant was his lack of consideration of a structure in which the horizon of the future and the horizon of the past are folded into each other. Their mutual folding does not just distinguish the despair over that is based in despair of from forms of manifestation in which dominates either the extension to the future—as in the case of the youth—or the recourse to the past—as in the case of the adult. The folding of times also contrasts with the structurally significant forms in which despair—as the first sign of mania— gets into the vortex of the future or—as beginning depression— into the vortex of the past. That the temporal structure of despair is not discussed in *The Sickness unto Death* is initially correct inasmuch as that state that despair naturally possesses is not a subject matter prior to its actualization in specific forms, either eidetic or empirical. But the objection seems justified also because *The Sickness unto Death* thus also neglects the structure that specifically distinguishes, in a temporal respect, the phenomenon described in it from the other negative phenomena classified in the history of freedom. In its original form, Kierkegaard's anxiety is pure anxiety of the future; it becomes an anxiety staring into the past as well only in the later stages of its metamorphosis.[123]

Inasmuch as Kierkegaard—in competition with his approach in the discussion of in despair to will and not to will to be oneself—assumes the despair over something, his starting point is far from that of Aquinas: the reference to the past of despairing over contrasts with the reference to the future of despairing of. However, according to *The Sickness unto Death*, as we know, despair over something dissolves into mere semblance. Kierkegaard, who bound the whole philosophy of existence to his pathos of the future, also sets his stakes on the future in his analysis of despair. What disappears in semblance for him is the suffering, and the truth that emerges with its disappearance is supposed to be an activity which, as such, proceeds into the future. Nonetheless, his further development of *desperatio* takes its course through the past. For future and past are not only folded into each other because the past-related despair over, which in itself is a semblance, has its truth in the future-related despair of. The mutual folding returns in a modified way in the despair of. In fundamental despair, we have even encountered a more extensive past. People usually despair over something that has just happened or something they have just learned of. Between the event that plunges them into despair and the current present, no more time needs to pass than is necessary for their despairing reaction. In fundamental despair, on the other hand, the past of what is always already past plays a role. Moreover, it increases in importance as it becomes part of the act of despairing itself rather than only defining its concrete correlate. For Kierkegaard traces despair over the earthly back to a despair of the eternal so that he tries to demonstrate: a person who despairs over something *is* already in despair, that is, in despair of the eternal. To despair of the eternal means to be, always already, in despair of it. The past recurring in fundamental despair is despair's own past. In it, future and past are folded into each other so that *as* an act referring to the future, fundamental despair reaches back into time immemorial. But that strengthens the significance of *desperatio* itself. The act that lets go of all hope turns out to be based in a hopelessness that has come over men—forever and from afar.

Kierkegaard develops the *desperatio* further by tripling it, as it were. He does this by increasingly deepening the foundation.

The first *desperatio* appears in his work under a pseudonym: it hides behind the despaired not willing to be oneself that we initially encounter beneath the surface of appearance. The second is encountered as soon as we descend from the level of structural forms to the level of the comprehensive structure: there it is veiled in the disguise of a despairing of the eternal, in which it is accommodated as an act of ridding oneself of hope. The third *desperatio*, finally, emerges from the depths of that hopelessness. That it is the heaviest burden becomes clear in its role in molding the reference to the future of the despair of the eternal. The despair of the eternal relates to the future only negatively. As despair of that which saves, it discloses the horizon of the future in such a way that it closes it *off*. But if we do not lose our trust in what saves us only just now, but have lost it always already, then the future is completely closed off to us. Then in our hopelessness, we may not hope that it will be open to us again. The hope for that dwindles, too, because the past of our despair—if we are not torn out of it—perpetuates itself into the future and demotes our hope to a quasi-past.

Perhaps from here, we can even find a good sense of Kierkegaard's judgment on true and seeming despair. He entrusts to seeming not really the reality that makes us despair, but rather the despairing as an ever-present something happening to us. The verdict becomes more plausible when it is interpreted as saying that it wants to destroy the appearance that despairing is a momentary issue. According to this reading, the person in despair understands himself properly only when he becomes aware that he has always already been in despair and will be in despair forever without outside intervention. Thus grasped, it would be absolutely reasonable to place true despair within the self. In the ever present event happening to him, the person in despair must bring his self before himself by realizing his desperation extending in time. Kierkegaard commits an irreparable error only insofar as he reinterprets the temporal self-presence as reflection, initially as the reflection of the despairing person, then as the reflection that changes the despair over something into despair over oneself. We have seen that Kierkegaard identifies despair of the eternal with despair over oneself. This identification in itself is completely unacceptable. But even this identification contains a genuine intuition. A person who despairs of the eternal plunges into the abyss of his despair. The despair recorded in the self-relation in such a way can indeed no longer be played off against the despair happening to oneself. It is in his desperation that the subject feels, above all, the power of what has already happened to him.

Summarizing Conclusion

Dialectic in The Sickness unto Death

1. Even today, a great many readers may still endorse the judgment that *The Sickness unto Death* "contains an extremely valuable psychological analysis of despair, which must however first be extricated from Kierkegaard's style trained in Hegelian dialectic. But then it is probably one of the best and most profound pieces that has ever been said or written about despair."[1] Incidentally, our contribution to the immanent critical reconstruction and transcending critique of the intrinsically valuable analysis of despair may seem to be an attempt to extricate it from its dialectical schema, and thus to take into account the fact that Kierkegaard himself felt that his book was "too dialectical."[2] However, in the same journal entry in which he expresses his discomfort, he also bears in mind that the book has enriched him with an "excellent plan"; and in the following entry, in which he considers the possibility of structuring the book "rhetorically," he finally tears himself away from this thought by raising the objection: "The dialectical algebra [*Bogstavregning*] works better."[3] But what is "the dialectical" of which he says that he must always have it thoroughly fluent before he begins using "the rhetorical"?[4] What do we have to understand by "Kierkegaard's style trained in Hegelian dialectic"? In general, people do not even have a highly determinate idea of Hegel's dialectic, and the vague picture of it is usually projected onto

Kierkegaard's dialectic so that it becomes an even vaguer mirror image. If someone such as Karl Popper brings Hegel's dialectic down to three steps of thesis, antithesis, and synthesis, Kierkegaard's is trimmed to two steps, which directly opposes the antithesis to a thesis, and no longer extends to a synthesis. These kinds of adaptations seldom go so far as to miss the issue completely, and thus there is also something true in the construct of an irreconcilable dialectic. But the relative truth content of that construct is revealed only by looking at what it diminishes and obstructs. And naturally, we must have a non-reductive concept of Kierkegaard's dialectic if only to be able to ask whether the immanent and the transcending critique of *The Sickness unto Death* exercised here releases his analysis of despair from its dialectical makeup.

Kierkegaard receives Hegel's extremely multilayered dialectic in almost as multilayered a fashion. Above all, he appropriates it in its epistemological-ontological ambiguity which characterized it in speculative thought, insofar as it was intended to be not only a method, but also an intrinsic structure of the real. Kierkegaard's "existential dialectic" is a variety, restricted to human existence, of what since Nicolai Hartmann is often called a "real dialectic." Just as in the speculative logic, the dialectic of being is different from that of essence and the dialectic of essence is in turn different from that of the concept, so, too, in the existential ethic, the real dialectic of human existence is differently constituted depending on the paths in which it moves. In *The Sickness unto Death*, Kierkegaard represents it by examining its various forms one after another. On the other hand, the dialectical method guides the entire method of his treatise. The method I have called "negativistic" is one part of that method, the most important part, which is itself a whole or is the whole method as is immediately relevant philosophically. The dialectical method extends over both parts of his book, the first which unfolds the philosophy of despair, and the second which moves this philosophy into the perspective of the theology of sin. The negativistic-dialectical method, on the other hand, especially determines the way Kierkegaard proceeds in the first section. The dialectical, which unites one method with the other, is that in both the greater and the smaller whole Kierkegaard begins with presuppositions he secures only in the further course of his analysis.[5] The whole conception is structured dialectically insofar as only the second part discusses the theological preliminary decisions made at the beginning. With that, the appearance dissolves as if the initial anthropology were given precedence—in the hardened shape of an independent introductory science—over theology. In light of the second part, it becomes clear that even the ostensibly purely anthropological statements of the exposition are to be read theologically. This technique of disclosure incorporates Hegel's argument that if the true is whole, the beginning can only be the untrue. The philosophical description is structured negativistic-dialectically insofar as only the analysis, following the exposition, of the negative phenomenon of despair justifies the initially merely asserted propositions on man, his self, and the established being of his self. Securing assumptions takes place here as a belated explanation of assertions. Here, too, an appearance disappears, that is, the appearance as if the initial theory of the self would provide an absolute criterion—in the grand form of an intrinsically evident fundamental philosophy—for the concrete analysis of the phenomenon. The course taken by the first part shows that the seemingly pure affirmative postulates of the exposition were really informed by the anticipatory view of the negative. An affirmation that conceals that it emerged from a negation of the negative is also untrue.

The methodological aspect of the dialectic invested in *The Sickness unto Death* has been illuminated more thoroughly elsewhere.[6] Here I would like to turn to its substantive aspect, to the dialectic as a real structure. In our text, we encounter an objective dialectic with three layers: first, in the anthropological approach as the law of being human, then in the first course through the forms of despair as the law that the renunciation of being human is subject to; and finally in the second course through those forms as the procedural law of that despair which becomes at once more conscious of itself and more intense.

2. The anthropological approach marks the place which Kierkegaard, far from the amputation he is often accused of, assigns to Hegel's positive dialectic. The synthesis discussed there is to be understood in a thoroughly Hegelian fashion as the execution of a unity which relates the "thesis" and "antithesis" with one another so that only in the process do they become what they are as elements of that unity. We have seen that finitude and infinitude, necessity and possibility, because they are synthesized, acquire a determinateness which they do not have as independent spheres. That Kierkegaard, confusingly enough, passes off the self as the "positive third,"[7] even though it is characterized by negativity, may be explained, last but not least, by his need to communicate with the reader about the mediatory achievement of the synthesis. The positive-dialectical constitution of human Dasein, in the Hegelian sense, emerges even more clearly when we consider that to demonstrate it in the phenomenon of despair is to change it somewhat, inasmuch as it also makes the elements of the synthesis dynamic. It is not only the three initially distinguished forms of despair that are revealed in retrospect as stages of a process. The ostensibly static structural elements are also dissolved into movements. Thus Kierkegaard again uses a dialectical procedure, that of "liquefaction" (Nicolai Hartmann). He liquefies infinitude to the infinitizing through which an individual gets away from himself in the projection of his possibility; he liquifies finitude to the finitizing process through which an individual comes back to himself in the necessity of the given situation.[8] But the synthesis is realized as the unity of these movements, as the itself processing reality of the Dasein, "getting away from" and "coming back to" itself.

3. In his first course through the forms of despair, Kierkegaard describes the deficiency of the synthesis as the failure of such a unity. The people he considers in despair do not even begin to get away from themselves or to come back to themselves; they are drowned in finitude or lose themselves in infinitude. With regard to Kierkegaard's conception of dialectic, we must be interested in how he moves from being human to failing it. The text explaining the proposition that to despair of infinitude is to lack finitude, and the complementary text commenting on the proposition that to despair of finitude is to lack infinitude, both begin with the assertion: "That this is so is due to the dialectic inherent in the self as a synthesis, and therefore each constituent is its opposite."[9] The opening of both discourses with an identical statement underscores the significance that Kierkegaard attaches to the "dialectical."[10] But what does he mean by it? *Prima facie*, he appeals to the structure of the human Dasein already introduced. If we take him at his word, he seems simply to want to say that the reciprocal dependency of the opposing elements is the condition of possibility for the failure of the double movement. If finitude were not formed into infinitude and infinitude were not formed into finitude in and through the synthesis, a life that wrests finitude from infinitude, or infinitude from finitude, could hardly be the phenomenon of lack, which it is on account of its one-sidedness. It is indeed striking that Kierkegaard speaks of one constituent and its opposite as Hegel speaks of the determinations of reflection. Secretly, he even combines two stages in the determinations of the definitions of reflection. It becomes clear from the further course of his analysis that he is thinking of a relation in which the one and the other constituent mutually reflect each other: each has its opposite in itself and can thus be defined only with regard to its opposite.[11] However, intrinsically, the dictum claims more: each *is* its opposite. In the speculative logic of the opposition, that relation of implication designates the starting point of a movement that drifts toward this change into one

another. Now the relation of implication can be depicted in the relation of the elements of the synthesis to one another, but the conversion cannot. Finitude and infinitude, necessity and possibility reflect each other in our being human, but they are not exchanged. Only in incongruity can both forms of opposition be discovered. The initial form is the one offered by the opposition of in despair not to will to be oneself and in despair to will to be oneself in the first course through the forms; the final form is the one assumed in the second course. In Kierkegaard's view, in despair to will to be oneself resides in desperately willing to be oneself, and, vice versa, in despair not to will to be oneself resides in desperately willing to be oneself. In the First Study, this dialectic was identified as that of a motivational overlap: not to will to be oneself contains willing to be oneself, insofar as we do not want to be what we are because we want to be what we are not; and to will to be oneself contains not willing to be oneself, insofar as we want to be what we are not because we do not want to be what we are. As has been shown, the chapter that seeks to grasp the forms of despair as antithetical unilateralist reductions of being human translates the motivational overlap into the anthropological realm. In all forms of our deficient existence, we do not want to be what we are as human beings, and want to be what we are not as human beings, so that the motivation for our not willing to be, the fear of the effort of being human, establishes the basis of the motivation for our willing to be, the yearning for the nonhuman—just as it is presumably this yearning which, in Kierkegaard's view, in turn provides the motivational basis for that fear. The chapter that dissolves the forms of despair in stages of a process, on the other hand, reinforces the dialectic. By transforming the opposition of in despair not to will to be oneself and in despair to will to be oneself into that of weakness and defiance, it also changes the form of the opposition itself. It at least tends to advance the claim that weakness *is* defiance, defiance *is* weakness. Weakness and defiance not only reflect one another, they convert into one another. Read literally, therefore, the repeated proposition, which is to explain the title proposition on the despair of infinitude and finitude, aims at the structure of a mutual relation that only weakness and defiance enter into. In this respect, this is a case of the reduplication of content in terms of form that Kierkegaard was striving for. Kierkegaard describes a real lack with the means of a deficient dialectic. The formal object of his morphology of despair is in fact an opposition, whose extremes are not mediated by a third element. Yet he arranges it so that, in the transition from being human to its failure, he retreats from the trichotomous dialectic of the concept to the dichotomous dialectic of essence or of reflection. In this retreat, the synthetic dialectic remains present as the structure that is destroyed by the renunciation of being human that is sketched according to the model of the catastrophic development of determinations of reflection.

We can now pause and take up the question of whether the immanent and transcending critique leaves the dialectical structure of *The Sickness unto Death* intact or demolishes it. It can certainly not spare it entirely or even restore it. After all, the demonstration in the First Study of the asymmetry in the relation of in despair not willing to be oneself and in despair willing to be oneself also shows that this relation is not that of a reciprocal implication. If it is possible that we do not will to be what we are, without willing to be what we are not, then not to will to be oneself does not, in any case, imply willing to be oneself in the same way as to will to be oneself implies not willing to be oneself. The insight into the asymmetry of the relation of weakness and defiance gained in the Second Study also reveals how far removed these are from mutually changing into one another. We not only need to deny that weakness *is* defiance and defiance *is* weakness. We also need to deny that weakness incorporates defiance to the same extent that defiance incorporates weakness. Between them, there is indeed a mutual implication, but merely an asymmetrical one. While weakness betrays an element of defiance only as the defined weakness of not willing to be oneself only in certain situations, defiance for its part is virtually based on weakness. However, from all that, it does not follow for our discussion of Kierkegaard's dialectic that we would have to bid farewell to it. Our results instruct us rather to evade the bad alternatives of conservation and dismantling. With Kierkegaard's dialectical interpretation of the phenomenon, it is the same situation as with his interpretation in general: it discloses and closes off at the same time. In the perspective of a dialectically constituted reality, Kierkegaard really sees something, despite all distortions and reductions. He can hardly be accused of merely toying with Hegel's dialectical figures of thought. That each constituent *is* it opposite may be an overly trenchant expression for what is meant; nevertheless, it is in the extended line of his descriptions. The seriousness with which he uses the instrument given him by Hegel is shown in his sure feeling for the limits of the applicability of this instrument. It is not that he would apply the Hegelian dialectic unrestrictedly to being human and its failure, and, in applying it thus, would merely reproduce it. Rather, he knows exactly where he reaches the point where any dialectic derived from Hegel fails because reality itself is no longer constituted in a purely dialectical fashion. However, it is all the more remarkable that he connects even this point with the speculative logic. He puts it in such a direct relation with it that it seems immaterial whether one wants to see behind the limit something other than dialectic or a different dialectic. The chapter on the deficient consummation of human Dasein is an impressive testimony to this, too.

The spiritual health that corresponds to the sickness in the spirit, according to this chapter, is "the ability to resolve contradictions."[12] The sentence is reminiscent of a comment by Hegel: "Something is therefore alive only in so far as it contains contradictions within it, and moreover is this power to hold and endure the contradiction within it."[13] However, in the quoted passage, Kierkegaard does not talk of his version of enduring, of holding together the extremes of being human. In his view, the synthesis is not an existing contradiction. He reserves the concept of contradiction for despair which, as a rupture, is nothing but an existential contradiction. Correspondingly, he conceives of health, which is achieved by resolving contradictions, as the health of faith.[14] But the special contradiction which in context he entrusts to faith is the contradistinction of two claims: "Everything is possible"—"Nothing is possible." In such a pro and contra, we encounter the contradiction of despair, insofar as in despair it initially looks as if everything is possible and then the insight breaks through that nothing is possible. It is faith that resolves the contradiction by holding on to the insight of the person who is drowning in necessity and by trusting, nevertheless, that everything is possible. This trust is paradoxical in the most literal sense, contrary to the opinion that this situation requires us to form. At this point, therefore, dialectic turns into a paradox. Starting from Hegel's pure dialectic, Kierkegaard advances to the paradoxical dialectic found only in his work. It can also be characterized as a paradox that leaves all dialectic behind. Nevertheless, it has its exact place where in the speculative logic the catastrophic development of the determination of reflection ends. The resolution of the contradiction through faith quotes the resolution of the contradiction that Hegel describes in the concluding section of the chapter on the determinations of reflection.[15] In a certain respect, this resolution is itself already paradoxical, because it is not a sub*lation*, being without the positive element of a preservation. The positive results from it not through the renewal of the old, which has completely destroyed itself, but through the intrusion of something new. By placing the resolution of the contradiction into the new beginning made by faith with its counter-factual breaking out of the prevailing situation, Kierkegaard only deepens the divide, if you like, that already separates the end of the event of reflection from the beginning with its ground in Hegel.

4. Hegel's logical dialectic is not only differentiated intrinsically as the dialectic of the logic of being, the logic of reflection, and the logic of the concept; it is also distinct from the phenomenological dialectic, which follows its own law. This law is the model for the procedural law stipulated by Kierkegaard's dialectic for the process pursued in the second course through the forms of despair.[16] Kierkegaard orients himself to *The Phenomenology of Spirit* in the second course initially for the simple reason that he is pondering a process of consciousness. But he also has a more specific motive for that. For, according to Hegel, the process that the "natural consciousness" goes through can "be regarded as the pathway of *doubt*, or more precisely as the way of despair."[17] Thus, in Hegel, Kierkegaard could even find a framework for the treatment of his special subject as staked out in the science of the experience of consciousness. Presumably, Hegel's own phenomenology of despair inspired him as much as Fichte's *Vocation of Man*, which starts with doubt and ends in faith. He unfolds the dialectic of consciousness *as such*, like Hegel, by tearing open the rift that exists between the self-conception of the subject and his real condition, forcing him to recognize this conflict and perceive his situation more completely. He investigates the genuine dialectic of the consciousness in *despair* by demonstrating—carefully following Hegel's instruction—how the subject increasingly totalizes the loss of meaning, which is a total loss from the beginning, even for itself, being blind to the truth, that in a certain sense it approximates the more deeply it becomes entangled in its untruth. In this process, a certain appearance resolves itself, that is, the distinctively phenomenological appearance of a self-deception of the subject. For Kierkegaard, it is the appearance as if despair were an event happening to oneself. The totalization realized by the subject occurs by virtue of a progressive transformation of suffering into activity. Thus the appearance is to resolve itself according to the Hegelian principle of a self-fulfilling mediation of immediacy. Finally, the engine driving the whole process

is removed from the vehicle of the speculative dialectic, too: the negativity. When Kierkegaard says that to reach the truth, one must go through every negativity,[18] he gives away the secret of *The Phenomenology of Spirit*.

However, the situation in the second course through the forms of despair is no different from that in the first: here, too, Kierkegaard applies a "small modification," as he would say ironically, to his model text, which takes into account his own interests. It is because he is concerned with the freedom of the subject involved in the process that he revokes the automatism, which, in Hegel, necessarily sublates the natural consciousness into absolute knowledge. How resolutely he thus creates room for his own interests is elucidated by a comparison of his reception of the Hegelian dialectic with its appropriation by Marx. Among the German neo-Hegelians, Marx was the only one to receive the Hegelian dialectic as comprehensively as Kierkegaard did. He, too, adheres to the real-dialectical claim; he also refuses to eliminate the contradiction from this dialectic; he also preserves the legacy of a thinking that destroys an ostensible immediacy and exposes mediating relations; and he also puts negativity as the driving force. The proximity of Marx and Kierkegaard becomes even more conspicuous in the fact that they share common ground in their respective ways of interpreting the idealistic scheme. Even in transforming the points mentioned they go partly in the same direction. Just consider the way they pluralize the contradiction into contradictions. In addition, they emphasize new aspects that also indicate a far-reaching agreement. In my study of Kierkegaard's negativistic method, I have pointed out that *The Sickness unto Death* uses the procedure of securing presuppositions in a way that is structurally similar to *Das Kapital*.[19] The distinction Marx makes in the preface to his major work between the "method of presentation" and the "method of inquiry"[20] aims at his methodological practice of reversing the course of inquiry in the presentation and starting with the outcome of his previous study of the material, with the highly mediated "value" and not with the obvious competition among private owners for means of production. Kierkegaard does something comparable when he puts at the beginning of his treatise the insights he has gained from his analysis of despair, in the form of his strong theses on man, the human self, and its established being. But even our examination here of how he degrades dialectic to the level of the determinations of reflections, for the sake of an appropriate presentation of the failure of synthesis, has a parallel in Marx. That Marx singles out the determinations of reflection so much among Hegel's dialectical figures of thought, in particular opposition and contradiction,[21] is explained by his conviction, linking him with Kierkegaard, that he is able to render real deficiencies only with correspondingly deficient means of thought. According to his maxim, an alienating social system has to be represented theoretically through determinations in which the unity of the concept has become alien to itself. In view of all these agreements, what is especially conspicuous is that Kierkegaard pursues his own path where Marx follows his philosophical master. Marx had blind faith in the automatism of a history that helps truth to triumph through all negativity. Kierkegaard, on the other hand, breaks the spell that petrifies history into an inevitable fate in Hegel.

While the consciousness Hegel observes is set to reach a destination inscribed within its concept and has to approach this destination on a prescribed route, the consciousness accompanied by Kierkegaard is confronted with alternatives at several stops along its way. To be sure, the possibilities that present themselves to consciousness are not arbitrary, nor are there as many as possible. To be precise, only two are designated and pictured explicitly. A person in despair can despair either progressively or regressively. Incidentally, Kierkegaard himself still describes these alternatives in dialectical terms. The movement forward leads into a certain truth recognized by Hegel as its own form of veritative being; it does not lead into the truth that, according to Kierkegaard, would be the completely other of despair, but into the truth *about* despair, into the manifestation of what despair is fundamentally all about. The movement backward reproduces the appearance from which it originates, the appearance of immediacy. It splits, for its part, into two possibilities, both of which are situated on the ground of immediacy, insofar as the person in despair is not in control of them. The difference between them corresponds exactly to the difference between pure immediacy and immediacy containing a quantitative reflection. If help comes from outside, the person in despair regains his happiness, which he thinks cures him of his sickness; if no help comes from outside, he sublimates his unhappiness, somewhat more reflectively, into a resignation in which he is satisfied to be one among others.[22] The innovation vis-à-vis Hegel's phenomenological dialectic is to admit such a retrograde step. However, aside from the two basic possibilities of a forward movement and a backward movement, Kierkegaard also hints at a third possibility, that is, of breaking sideways out of the path of a permanent intensification of despair and daring the leap into faith. But he does not designate it explicitly as a possibility obviously because, in his view, it cannot be a possibility for the individual in despair itself as long as it is still on its way.[23] At this point, it becomes clear that the ring of dialectic that Kierkegaard wraps around his analysis of processualizing despair is also a shackle. His variant of a phenomenological critique is exposed to critique not because he agrees with Hegel, who identifies the beginning as the wrapped-up end and the end as the unwrapped beginning. Both the immanent and transcending critique were based on the thoroughly Hegelian thesis that the beginning vouches for the primordial only insofar as the whole does indeed complete itself in it. To place the origin, which still conceals itself in the beginning and comes to light only at the end, into something other than Kierkegaard does is in no way to replace it. Nor does distancing oneself from the view that the initial appearance was an event happening to oneself also deny the fundamental principle that it is a misapprehension in the appearance that prevents the primordial from showing itself in its truth at the very beginning. No, what evokes a critique is the presupposition in Kierkegaard's rejection of that third possibility. The leap sideways is not a possibility for the person in despair himself, because what Kierkegaard does state clearly enough is considered a forgone conclusion: to reach the truth, one must go through *every* negativity.

Kierkegaard drags this presupposition along as the Hegelian he secretly always was and as he emerged even more often after 1846.[24] A remnant of automatism remains preserved in his theory, insofar as it does not relieve the consciousness seeking to avoid a relapse of completing its workload. Kierkegaard thus thwarts his own intention to emphasize freedom. The break with his intention is expressed, like others, in a violation of language. The joy of reading *The Sickness unto Death* is spoiled mainly because the book is composed in a language that mystifies its subject matter by substituting the real subjects with the self, on the one hand, and despair on the other. Both those hypostatizations result in stylistic absurdities. It is absurd that it is not the concrete person, but rather his self that is to relate to itself, reflect on itself, or lose itself; and it is even more absurd that there is a despair which, to take only two examples from passages quoted, is ignorant of having a self or lets itself be tricked out of itself by "the others."[25] The self owes its position as subject in dozens of sentences to the expansion of its concept reprimanded in the First Study: once it has assumed the appearance of the pre-given Dasein of an individual, it can easily slip into that individual's role. Despair can inflate into the ostensible subject because a dialectic that, in the punishment of regression, condemns one to endure the process of sickness to the very end absorbs the real subjects. As a residue of an unintended Hegelianism, however, this dialectic is not the one promised by the installation of alternatives. Perhaps it is not that there is too much dialectic invested in *The Sickness unto Death*, but too little, too little of the dialectic of the freedom that leaps out. But it can also be that, in coming into contact with such a freedom, dialectical thought comes up against its limit. Here, the uncertainty recurs of whether paradox establishes a different dialectic or refers to something other than dialectic. For leaping out of the path of disaster, this premature leap into faith, as it were, would be as paradoxical as faith itself, which unties the knot by cutting it.

Notes

Preface

1. In a journal record that is left us in his "Papers" (see the Summarizing Conclusion). I cite here the *Papirer*, ed. by P. A. Heiberg and V. Kuhr (Copenhagen, 1909–48), with Roman (and, if necessary, Arabic) numerals for the volume number, capital letters for the section, and Arabic numerals for the number of the entry. Here: Pap. VIII A 651.

2. I became aware of him through an excellent lecture at the conference in Aarhus mentioned below. See George Pattison, *Kierkegaard: The Aesthetic and the Religious* (Basingstoke/Hampshire: Macmillan, 1992).

3. *Der Begriff Ernst bei Søren Kierkegaard*, dissertation, Freiburg i. Br., 1955; published in 1958 in Verlag Karl Alber as Vol. I of the series *Symposion*, 3rd ed. (1982).

4. See Pap. X 5 B 18.

5. Pap. X 5 B 25.

6. The follow-up lecture was given by Alastair Hannay ("Notes on Kierkegaard's Notion of Wanting in Despair to Be Oneself"). Hannay represented the counter-thesis corresponding to Kierkegaard's self-conception that authentic despair was that one despairs of wanting to be oneself. This is not the place to get into his subtle objections, except for one point. The discussion with Hannay has taught me that it is wise to establish more clearly: in the first study, to a large extent, I describe not Kierkegaard's intention, but rather his actual thought process, what Kierkegaard actually does—now and then against his stated intention.

7. Michael Theunissen, "Kierkegaard's Negativistic Method," in Joseph H. Smith (ed.), *Kierkegaard's Truth: The Disclosure of the Self*,

Psychiatry and the Humanities, vol. 5 (New Haven and London: Yale University Press, 1981), 381–423.

8. M. Theunissen, *Das Selbst auf dem Grund der Verzweiflung. Kierkegaards negativistische Methode* (Frankfurt a.M.: Anton Hain, 1991).

First Study: The Existential Dialectical Basic Assumption of Kierkegaard's Analysis of Despair

1. All quotations are from Søren Kierkegaard, *The Sickness unto Death: A Christian Psychological Exposition for Upbuilding and Awakening*, ed. and trans. Howard V. Hong and Edna Hong (Princeton: Princeton University Press, 1980). I should add that in what follows, I consider the semi-pseudonymous treatise allegedly written by Anti-Climacus and edited by Kierkegaard to be Kierkegaard's own work. By attributing it to a pseudonym (which he added only later), Kierkegaard only meant to suggest that he had not personally attained the level of belief by which Anti-Climacus measures human life. As for its content, Kierkegaard's identification with his treatise is unqualified.

2. Such an approach is at least not inadequate to the text since Kierkegaard claims to present "a consistently developed basic view" (p. 22).

3. "Despair is a Sickness of the Spirit, of the self, and accordingly can take three forms: in despair not to be conscious of having a self (not despair in the strict sense), in despair not to will to be oneself; in despair to will to be oneself" (13). See Johannes Hohlenberg, "Sygdommen til Døden. Et exempel paa Søren Kierkegaards psykologiske syn," *Samtiden* 52 (1941): 358–369, esp. 361: "These words, which stand as a heading for the first chapter of the book, give the essential content, and what follows is only a closer development of what is to be understood by these expressions."

4. The "internal arrangement" is to be examined in the Second Study.

5. See Michael Theunissen, "Das Menschenbild in der *Krankheit zum Tode*," in M. Theunissen and W. Greve (eds.), *Materialien zur Philosophie Søren Kierkegaards* (Frankfurt a.M., 1979), 469–509; Michael Theunissen, *Das Selbst auf dem Grund der Verzweiflung. Kierkegaards negativistische Methode* (Frankfurt a.M., 1991).

6. The methodological abstraction from the theological preliminary decisions implies that I am largely disregarding the second part of *The Sickness unto Death*. Thus, the subject of both studies united here is the thesis that "the sickness unto death is despair," not so much the thesis that "despair is the sin." This also means that "the theologi-

cal self, the self directly before God" (79) here remains necessarily under-determined.

7. See *Das Selbst auf dem Grund der Verzweiflung*.

8. "The self is a relation that relates itself to itself or is the relation's relating itself to itself in the relation; the self is not the relation but is the relation's relating itself to itself" (13). See M. Theunissen, "Das Menschenbild in der *Krankheit zum Tode*," loc. cit. (note 5), 498; and M. Theunissen, *Das Selbst auf dem Grund der Verzweiflung*, loc. cit. (note 5), II.2.3, "Das Selbst as substratloser Prozess" (51–57).

9. In *Die Verzweiflung als metaphysisches Phänomen in der Philosophie Søren Kierkegaards* (Würzburg, 1934), Bernhard Meerpohl places the analysis of despair in the context of the Kierkegaardian dialectic of existence. Meerpohl sees despair primarily as an evasion of the transition into the higher sphere of existence (see esp. pp. 42–43). In what follows, the relation to the various stages will be omitted. Most of the material for that is contained in the otherwise scanty section on the despair that is ignorant of being despair (1, C, B, a). See the recent work by Wilfried Greve, "Wo bleibt das Ethische in Kierkegaards *Krankheit zum Tode*?" in E. Angehrn, H. Fink-Eitel, Ch. Iber, and G. Lohmann (eds.), *Dialektischer Negativismus* (Frankfurt a.M., 1992), 323–341.

10. For the dialectic in *The Sickness unto Death*, see the conclusion.

11. The reconstruction attempted here would not be one if all it took were simply to pick up what Kierkegaard said himself. That we do not will to be what we are is nowhere expressed like that in *The Sickness unto Death*, let alone formulated as "a fundamental principle" [*Grundsatz*].

12. From the fact that Socrates is "not an essentially religious ethicist, even less a Christian dogmatician," Kierkegaard concludes: "Therefore he does not really enter into the whole investigation with which Christianity begins, into the *prius* [antecedent state] in which sin presupposes itself and which is explained in Christianity in the dogma of hereditary sin, the border of which this discussion will merely approach" (89).

13. For the distinction between the first and second ethics, see *The Concept of Anxiety* (CA), ed. and trans. Reidar Thomte (Princeton: Princeton University Press, 1980), 16–24; for the parallel with Schelling's distinction between negative and positive philosophy, see CA, 21 note.

14. I distinguish between the being established by God and being established as such. See *Das Selbst auf dem Grund der Verzweiflung*, loc. cit, (note 5), II.2.I (35–38).

15. We are pre-given to ourselves as Dasein "in this specific concretion of relations" (68). The much complained-of "akosmism" of *The Sickness unto Death* is an invention of its interpreters.

16. Kierkegaard prefers a Hegelianizing concept of "nothing" (see *inter alia*, 25, 69–70). But according to his treatise on anxiety, the "nothing" after all is indeterminateness, the nothing of a spirit, *to* which the individual is determined in the state of innocence, but *as* which it is not yet determined.

17. Instead of the abstract self, *The Sickness unto Death* also talks of the "infinite form of the negative self" (68). Behind that is the view that the abstract self is only its "first form." On the other hand, I plead for the concept of self to be restricted to the abstract self.

18. Or in his own words: "this very specific being with these natural capacities, predispositions, etc." (68). In contast to "this naked and abstract self," Kierkegaard also talks of the "immediacy's fully dressed self" (55).

19. Every individual has "to be itself in its essential contingency" (33).

20. Thus, for example, he says of a person, "that the self he is is a very definite something, and thus the necessary" (36).

21. See the second part of the section on the despair, 69–74.

22. "A person in despair despairingly wills to be himself [. . .] The self that he despairingly wants to be is a self that he is not (for the will to be the self that he is in truth is the very opposite of despair) . . ." (20).

23. "The self is so far from successfully becoming more and more itself that the fact merely becomes increasingly obvious that it is a hypothetical self" (69). Whoever wants despairingly to be himself in the way described at the outset wants "to be master of itself or to create itself into the self he wants to be, to determine what he will have or not have in his concrete self" (68).

24. For the dissolution into an abstraction, see the remarks on infinitude's despair (30–33). Kierkegaard emphasizes mainly the secondary status of the wish to be someone else. Of the despair to which the "immediate self" succumbs when no help comes from outside, he says: "This form of despair is: in despair not to will to be oneself. Or even lower: in despair not to will to be a self. Or lowest of all: in despair to will to be someone else, to wish for a new self" (52–53). What is wished in such a wish is the "most lunatic of lunatic metamorphoses" (53). However, that sentence is also one of the nonsensical sentences in *The Sickness unto Death*. Aside from the unreasonableness of the premise, according to which in despair not to will to be oneself is low, it appears incomprehensible why in despair not to will to be a self is even lower, since, in Kierkegaard's own view, everyone in despair wants to get rid

of his self, and what is least satisfying is that when Kierkegaard degrades the wish to be someone else to the lowest form of despairingly not willing to be oneself, he levels the difference between this and despairingly willing to be oneself.

25. After Kierkegaard has contrasted the self as established by an Other against an establishment of self, he continues: "The human self is such a derived, established relation, a relation that relates itself to itself and in relating itself to itself relates itself to another. This is why there can be two forms of despair in the strict sense. If a human self had itself established itself, then there could be only one form: not to will to be oneself, to will to do away with oneself, but there could not be the form: in despair to will to be oneself" (13–14).

26. Something of this interest becomes apparent in the following remark: "Similarly, the eternal in a person can be proved by the fact that despair cannot consume his self, that precisely this is the torment of contradiction in despair" (21). How "the eternal in a person" relates to God is discussed in the Second Study, IV, 2 and 3.

27. The person raging in the most extreme despair of defiance wants "to tear itself loose from the power which established it, for spite wants to force itself upon it, to obtrude defiantly upon it, wants to adhere to it out of malice—and, of course, a spiteful denunciation must above all take care to adhere to what it denounces" (72).

28. Kierkegaard tackles this in his second course through the forms of despair oriented toward the level of consciousness (49ff., 67ff.).

29. In his hypostatizing language: the most intensive form of despair does "not even in defiance or defiantly will to be itself, but for spite" (73).

30. The revolt against God is to be distinguished from that against fate. See Max Sack, *Die Verzweiflung. Eine Untersuchung ihres Wesens und ihrer Entstehung*. And an appendix: Søren Kierkegaard's "Krankheit zum Tode," Kallmünz 1930, Phil. diss., Munich, 1929, pp. 7–8, 36–40. It is striking that, in his discussion of rebellious defiance, Kierkegaard often substitutes "Dasein" for God. The rebel in despair "has convinced himself that this thorn in the flesh gnaws so deeply that he cannot abstract himself from it [. . .] in spite of or in defiance of all existence, he wills to be himself, takes it along, almost flouting his agony" (70–71). As the "wronged victim of the whole world and of all life" (72), as he feels himself, he is filled with "hatred toward existence" and "rebelling against all existence," he feels that he "has obtained evidence against it and its goodness" (73). Perhaps Kierkegaard gives the revolt against God the appearance of a revolt against the ontologi-

cal face of destiny, that is, "Dasein," because in this garb he can project it more easily back onto more elementary forms of despair.

31. "Yes, this second form of despair (in despair to will to be oneself) is so far from designating merely a distinctive kind of despair that, on the contrary, all despair ultimately can be traced back to and be resolved in it" (14). "To despair over oneself, in despair to will to be rid of oneself—this is the formula for all despair. Therefore the other form of despair, in despair to will to be oneself, can be traced back to the first, in despair not to will to be oneself, just as we previously resolved the form, in despair not to will to be oneself into the form, in despair to will to be oneself" (20).

32. Whether there is even a fourth form to be added depends on the interpretation of the sentence: "No despair is entirely free of defiance; indeed the very phrase 'not to will to be' implies defiance" (49). See the Second Study, II.2.

33. The demonic despair, whose subject does not break free of God, but rather wants to force itself on Him, is no longer characterized by the same will for the impossible that is implicit in the previous forms of despair. There may no longer be any will of the impossible in it. It is more likely that something new is involved in it, that which is necessarily linked with the perversion of not being in despair. For this perversion, see II.4.

34. "A person cannot rid himself of the relation to himself any more than he can rid himself of his self, which, after all, is one and the same thing, since the self is the relation to oneself" (17). Thus, despair is "the hopelessness of not even being able to die," "an impotent self-consuming that cannot do what it wants to do," this tormenting contradiction, this sickness of the self, perpetually to be dying, to die and yet not die, to die death" (18).

35. Thus, the title of section C, B, a (which hypostasizes despair such that it substitutes despair for the person in despair): "The Despair that is ignorant of being despair, or the despairing ignorance of having a Self and an eternal Self" (42). Kierkegaard describes inauthentic despair mainly as one in which man is not conscious of *it* (see, inter alia, 21, 23).

36. The theme of the passages about the despair of weakness and of defiance is "a rise in the consciousness of the nature of despair and in the consciousness that one's state is despair, or, what amounts to the same thing and is the salient point, a rise in the consciousness of the self" (49).

37. Thus, the thesis of the "universality" of despair (22–28) becomes questionable. For Kierkegaard tries to justify this universality with the

assumption of an unconscious despair. But he can produce the appearance as if there were a despair in which the person does not know that he is in a state of despair, only by taking the way through anxiety and identifying it, against his better judgment, with despair. Even deep within happiness, he says, there dwells anxiety (22), "which is despair" (25). See 44: "The relation between ignorance and anxiety (cf. *The Concept of Anxiety* by Vigilius Harniensis); the anxiety that characterizes spiritlessness is recognized precisely by its spiritless sense of security. Nevertheless, anxiety lies underneath; likewise, despair also lies underneath, and when the enchantment of illusion is over, when existence begins to totter, then despair, too, immediately appears as that which lay underneath." For the difference between anxiety and anxiety in despair, see M. Sack, *Die Verzweiflung*, op. cit. (note 30), 9–15.

38. A critique of the assumption of an unconscious despair has been presented before. See M. Sack, op. cit., 133; Hildegard Kraus, "Verzweiflung und Selbstsein. Zum Ersten Abschnitt der *Krankheit zum Tode*," *Kierkegaardiana* 13 (1984): 45. But first the objective of the critique remains vague because the different meanings of the concept of an unconscious despair are not distinguished; and second, the critique is also unfair because it omits Kierkegaard's own reservations. In no other point was Kierkegaard so unsure of his case as in the question of an unconscious despair. At the beginning of his investigation of the consciousness of despair, he states with striking indecisiveness: "Despair at its minimum is a state that—yes, one could humanly be tempted almost to say that in a kind of innocence it does not even know that it is despair. There is the least despair when this kind of consciousness is greatest; it is almost a dialectical issue whether it is justifiable to call such a state despair" (42). In the passage on that despair, which Kierkegaard later characterizes as conscious on the background of the unconscious one, he himself makes a qualification: "Actual life is too complex merely to point out abstract contrasts as that between a despair that is completely unaware of being so and a despair that is completely aware of being so" (48). As early as the opening paragraphs to the entire section on the forms of despair, it reads: "Granted, all despair regarded in terms of the concept is conscious, but this does not mean that the person who, according to the concept, may appropriately be said to be in despair, is conscious of it himself" (29). The differentiation, which is hard to understand if taken for itself, is not sufficiently explicated to be interpretable unequivocally. Perhaps we may understand the concession that, in terms of its concept, all despair is conscious as acknowledgment of the fact mentioned below

that a person in despair must be conscious of himself "in the sense of an accompanying self-presence."

39. Kierkegaard aims at such despair with sentences like these: "But to be unaware of being defined as spirit is precisely what despair is" (25). "An individual is furthest from being conscious of himself as spirit when he is ignorant of being in despair. But precisely this—not to be conscious of oneself as spirit—is despair, which is spiritlessness, whether the state is a thoroughgoing moribundity, a merely vegetative life, or an intense, energetic life, the secret of which is still despair" (44–45).

40. In the introductory sentence (see note 3), which reads: "in despair not to be conscious of having a self (not despair in the strict sense)."

41. Also, Kierkegaard imagines it as only a despair that is hardly noticeable affectively—and this must be considered in the discussion of his universality thesis: "The conclusion was not drawn that a person who is not in a more intensive state of despair is therefore not in despair. On the contrary, it was specifically shown that by far the great majority of men are in despair, but to a lesser degree" (101).

42. See the passages referred to in note 30. This kind of defiance is not congruent with the entire scope of defiance, interpreted by Kierkegaard as in despair to will to be oneself. It is the second, more mediated form of this defiance. The first form is the defiance of one who wants to be what he is not: "he does not want to put on his own self, does not want to see his given self as his task—he himself wants to compose his self by means of being the infinite form" (68).

43. The distinction not accommodated in the introductory proposition comes into play for the first time in Section A, C (18ff.). Kierkegaard picks it up (or thinks he does) with the distinction between a despair about something earthly (50ff.) and a despair of the eternal (60ff.), which he identifies with the one about oneself as a despair over one's own weakness. All this is the focus of the Second Study.

44. Starting from the inauthentic as the least intensive despair, the process is at once one of increasing intensity, which Kierkegaard very problematically equates with the idea that despair increasingly manifests itself externally. At times, the difference between weakness and defiance seems nearly congruent with that between covertness and manifestation. But even from this aspect, the investigation of degrees of awareness unfolds only what is already implicitly in the fundamental outline. See the conclusion of B: "Eternity asks you and every individual in these millions of millions about only one thing: whether you have lived in despair or not, whether you have despaired in such a way

that you did not realize that you were in despair, or in such a way that you covertly carried sickness inside of you as your gnawing secret, as a fruit of sinful love under your heart, or in such a way that you, a terror to others, raged in despair" (27–28).

45. Kierkegaard himself does not ask about the motives. Nor is the longing discussed below a subject for him.

46. In the *Concluding Unscientific Postcript,* Kierkegaard says drastically that "An existence of this sort is of a different order from the existence of a potato, but neither is it the kind of existence that attaches to an Idea" (VII 319). See M. Theunissen, "Das Menschenbild in der *Krankheit zum Tode,*" op. cit. (note 5), 503. For Kierkegaard's interpretation of the synthesis as one of ideality and reality, see Helmut Fahrenbach, *Kierkegaards existenzdialektische Ethik* (Frankfurt a.M., 1968), 14–15.

47. "When feeling becomes fantastic in this way, the self becomes only more and more volatilized and finally comes to be a kind of abstract sentimentality that inhumanly belongs to no human being but inhumanly combines sentimentality, as it were, with some abstract fate—for example, humanity *in abstracto*" (31).

48. This is significant for the assessment in the third section of this study of Kierkegaard's contribution to the preparation of Sartre's phenomenological ontology. In particular, the regressive tendency to become a thing is already marked out in *The Sickness unto Death,* which represents as it were the degenerate form of longing to become God in *L'être et le néant.*

49. See note 31.

50. "The inability of despair to consume him is so remote from being any kind of comfort to the person in despair that it is the very opposite. This comfort is precisely the torment, is precisely what keeps the gnawing alive and keeps life in the gnawing, for it is precisely over this that he despairs (not as having despaired): that he cannot consume himself, cannot get rid of himself, cannot reduce himself to nothing. This is the formula for despair raised to a higher power, the rising fever in this sickness of the self" (18–19). For the variously modified and adapted figure of thought of "raising to a higher power" in the text, see 42, 71, 77, 99, 108.

51. "This is an intensification, or the law of intensification" (18).

52. As in his "formula for all despair" (20).

53. Recall the phrase in parentheses in the sentence about the person who in despair wants to be a self he is not: "to will to be the self that he is in truth is the very opposite of despair" (20).

54. See M. Theunissen, *Das Selbst auf dem Grund der Verzweiflung, Kierkegaards negativistische Methode*, loc. cit., esp. 16ff.

55. To become a believer is to humble oneself "in adoration under the extraordinary" (86; see 78).

56. In the Second Study, we shall see that what underlies this spite is a suffering under something that is part of one's own existence. With reference to that, Kierkegaard writes: "Although suffering under it, the self will still not make the admission that it is part of the self, that is, the self will not in faith humble itself under it" (70n).

57. "As soon as despair becomes apparent, it is manifest that the individual was in despair. Hence, at no moment is it possible to decide anything about a person who has not been by having been in despair" (24). The awareness of existing with one's own self before God is "an infinite benefaction that is never gained except through despair" (27; see 30–31). Kierkegaard establishes the general principle: "to reach the truth, one must go through every negativity" (44).

58. See Book I of Plato's *Politics* (352d2–354ae) and chapter 6 of Aristotle's *Nichomachean Ethics* (1097b22–1098a20).

59. Kierkegaard follows the maxim: "the self must be broken in order to become itself" (65).

60. Jaspers, who is the existentialist philosopher closest to the Dane, is also the only one who directly adopted the philosophy of despair. See, esp., his *Psychologie der Weltanschauungen* (Berlin 1919), "Referat Kierkegaards." Moreover, independent of despair, he is strongly oriented toward the distinction of weakness and defiance. Finally, note that the proposal presented here to expand the anthropological approach of *The Sickness unto Death* toward the pre-given Dasein takes up in a certain respect the difference between existence and Dasein elaborated by Jaspers.

61. For Heidegger's use of the expressions "existential" and "existentiell," see William J. Richardson, *Heidegger: Through Phenomenology to Thought*, 3rd ed. (The Hague, 1974), 77–84.

62. See M. Theunissen, *Das Selbst auf dem Grund der Verzweiflung*, loc. cit., 35ff., 51ff.

63. Martin Heidegger, *Being and Time*, trans. John Macquarrie and Edward Robinson (New York, 1962), 32–33: "Dasein is an entity which does not just occur among other entities. Rather it is ontically distinguished by the fact that, in its very Being, that Being is an *issue* for it. But in that case, this is a constitutive state of Dasein's Being, and this implies that Dasein, in its Being, has a relationship towards that Being [. . .] That kind of Being towards which Dasein can comport itself in one way or another, and always does comport itself somehow,

we call '*existence*.' And because we cannot define Dasein's essence by citing a 'what' of the kind that pertains to a subject-matter, and because its essence lies rather in the fact that in each case it has its Being to be, and has as its own, we have chosen to designate this entity as 'Dasein,' a term which is purely an expression of its Being." Precisely there, Heidegger introduces the term of existentiality—which is ambiguous, in that it functions not only as a title for the self's relating itself to itself, but also stands for the structure of the whole. In the fifth chapter of Division One, he explicates the "Have-to-be" in terms of facticity.

64. See *Being and Time*, 67: "*The 'essence' of Dasein lies in its existence*" (emphasis in original).

65. "We are ourselves the entities to be analyzed. The Being of any such entity is *in each case mine*. These entities, in their being, comport themselves towards their Being. As entities with such Being, they are delivered over to their own being" (*Being and Time*, 67). And see *Being and Time*: "The expression 'thrownness' is meant to suggest the *facticity of its being delivered over*" (174).

66. The anthropological approach of *The Sickness unto Death* is based on this assumption: "The self *is* reflection" (31, emphasis M.T.). Kierkegaard was unable to bring this assumption into a coherent accord with the other one that posits that the self is will. He is content to assert a relation of implication between self-consciousness conceived as reflection and the will, which, as one that is identical with the self, has to be more original than the willing in being in despair and not being in despair: "Generally speaking, consciousness—that is, self-consciousness—is decisive with regard to the self. The more consciousness, the more self; the more consciousness, the more will; the more will, the more self. A person who has no will at all is not a self; but the more will he has, the more self-consciousness he has also" (29).

67. Or with everydayness. The difference between inauthenticity and the everyday, a very important one, can be neglected here. It has often been noted that Heidegger has a tendency to level this distinction in the course of his work. After everydayness has initially been defined as undifferentiated with regard to authenticity and inauthenticity, the beginning of the second division says: "In starting with average everydayness, our Interpretation has heretofore been confined to the analysis of such existing as is either undifferentiated or inauthentic" (275–276).

68. See the section on the despair of finitude, which says, for example: "But whereas one kind of despair plunges wildly in the infinite and loses itself, another kind of despair seems to permit itself to be tricked out of itself by 'the others.' Surrounded by hordes of men, absorbed

in all sorts of secular matters, more and more shrewd about the ways of the world—such a person forgets himself, forgets his name divinely understood, does not dare to believe in himself, finds it too hazardous to be himself and far easier and safer to be like the others, to become a copy, a number, a mass man" (33–34). This willing to be like the others is to be sharply distinguished from the despaired wish to be an other—more sharply than Kierkegaard occasionally does. Whereas with this wish one wants to be oneself in the sense that one wants to be what one is not, the imitation of others would have to be assigned to the not willing to be oneself. We are dealing here not only with the difference between the determinate other and the indeterminate others, but also with that between imaginary and empirical reality. The determinate other, on which the individual who arrogantly constructs himself remodels his Dasein, is imagined as a filler for the "hypothetical self," while the undefined others are taken from the bad reality.

69. Whoever has become "a number instead of a self, just one more man, just one more repetition of this everlasting *Einerlei* [one and the same]" (35), according to Kierkegaard, is also one of those "who, so to speak, mortgage themselves to the world" (35). Naturally, this expression is dictated by a New Testament understanding of the world. But, as we have learned from Hans Jonas, Heidegger also had a Gnostic, if not a biblical, understanding of the world.

70. "Dasein's absorption in the 'they' and its absorption in the 'world' of its concerns, make manifest something like a *fleeing* of Dasein in the face of itself—of itself as an authentic potentiality-for-Being-its-Self" (*Being and Time*, 229).

71. It is the function of Section V.1 of the Second Study to separate real despair from the chaff of a merely nominal despair in a more precise reading of this text.

72. "We call this everyday and undifferentiated character of Dasein *'averageness'* " (*Being and Time*, 69). When it is identified as Kierkegaard's "generality," provided that this was in fact considered as averageness.

73. Of course, by saying that, *in this point*, Kierkegaard is right as opposed to Heidegger; I do not mean to assert that Kierkegaard is right in every respect. But the most fundamental objection his existential ethics is open to (if we disregard its historical necessity), the objection raised in the first section of the Second Study, of the voidness of his existential ideal, is much more relevant even to Heidegger. In the perspective of this critique, Adorno's life-long debate with Kierkegaard should be included. For what Adorno finds fault with the existential dialectician—not only in his book on Kierkegaard of 1933, but also in his *Negative Dialectics*—is ultimately that any philosophy of the self remains empty of content.

74. "This existentiell-ontical turning-away, by reason of its character as a disclosure, makes it phenomenally possible to grasp existential-ontologically that in the face of which Dasein flees, and to grasp it as such." "When in falling we flee *into* the 'at-home' of publicness, we flee *in the face of* the 'not-at-home'; that is, we flee in the face of the uncanniness which lies in Dasein—in Dasein as thrown Being-in-the-world, which has been delivered over to itself in its Being" (*Being and Time*, 229 and 234).

75. Even in the "existential projection of anticipation," Heidegger declares in the chapter on death, we have clung "to those structures of Dasein which we have arrived at earlier, and we have, as it were, let Dasein itself project itself upon this possibility, without holding up to Dasein an idea of existence with any special 'content,' or forcing any such ideal upon it 'from outside'" (*Being and Time*, 311).

76. "Is there not, however, a definite ontical way of taking authentic existence, a factical ideal of Dasein, underlying our ontological interpretation of Dasein's existence? That is so indeed. But not only is this Fact one which must not be denied and which we are forced to grant; it must also be conceived in its *positive necessity*, in terms of the object which we have taken as the theme of our investigation" (*Being and Time*, 358).

77. The point at which Heidegger departs from Kierkegaard is that at which he moves toward a pre-fascist ideology. The negativity is replenished by an ideal of existence, which the author in reality takes from certain tendencies of his time. See Jürgen Habermas, *Philosophical Discourse of Modernity*, trans. Frederick G. Lawrence (Cambridge, Mass.: MIT Press, 1987), 157: "All the existential categories stay the same and yet with one stroke they change their very meaning—and not just the horizon of their expressive significance. The connotations they owe to their Christian origins, especially Kierkegaard, are transformed in the light of a New Paganism prevalent at that time."

78. So far, there has been no satisfactory examination of Heidegger's negativistic approaches. One of the few who has paid attention to them is W. Richardson in a lecture on "Die Gründung: Dasein and Negativity," delivered at the North American Heidegger conference in 1991 (Nashville, Tennessee). I am grateful to Stephen Cho of Yale University for letting me look at the underlying texts and notes to that lecture.

79. For the following, see the chapter on "Bad Faith," in Jean-Paul Sartre, *Being and Nothingness*, trans. Hazel E. Barnes (New York: Washington Square Press, 1966), 86–116.

80. The first sentence of the chapter on *mauvaise foi* is: "The human being is not only the being by whom *négatités* are disclosed in the

world; he is also the one who can take negative attitudes with respect to himself."

81. "Despair is the misrelation in the relation of synthesis that relates itself to itself" (15).

82. See *Being and Nothingness*, 120–121.

83. See *Being and Nothingness*, 36ff., and M. Theunissen, "Sartres negationstheoretische Ontologie der Zeit und Phänomenologie der Zeitdimensionen," in *Negative Theologie der Zeit*, 2nd ed. (Frankfurt a.M., 1992), 131–193, esp. 135ff.

84. For this, see especially the "Metaphysical Implications" at the end of the book (*Being and Nothingness*, 785ff.). Here, Sartre compares the "maladie de l'être" with the even worse disease from which the "for-itself" suffers; in a certain sense, it is a new form of "the sickness unto death."

SECOND STUDY: ON THE TRANSCENDING CRITIQUE
OF KIERKEGAARD'S ANALYSIS OF DESPAIR

1. This is inherent in the interpretation of despair as sin, the subject of the second part of *The Sickness unto Death*.

2. That is mainly to be seen in the critical picture the ethicist gives of the despair of his aesthetically living friend. See, e.g., *Either/Or* II, ed. and trans. Howard V. Hong and Edna H. Hong (Princeton, N.J.: Princeton University Press, 1987), 198: "You continually hover above yourself, but the higher atmosphere, the more refined sublimate, into which you are vaporized, is the nothing of despair" (179).

3. The "consistently developed basic view" (22)—which the conception of despair in *The Sickness unto Death* claims to be—builds on a classificatory principle which is supposed to encompass "the entire actuality of despair" (49–50n). However, where Kierkegaard describes the despair of weakness as feminine and the despair of defiance as masculine, he makes a qualification that is also to be taken into consideration: "I am far from denying that women may have forms of masculine despair and, conversely, that men may have forms of feminine despair but these are exceptions. And of course the ideal is also a rarity, and only ideally is this distinction between masculine and feminine despair altogether true" (49n). According to his own conception, Kierkegaard's "classification" is based on the construction of an ideal type.

4. "An individual in despair despairs over *something*. So it seems for a moment, but only for a moment; in the same moment the true despair

or despair in its true form shows itself. In despairing over *something*, he despaired over *himself*, and now he wants to be rid of himself" (19).

5. The passage is subdivided into two subsections. The first (50–60) is titled "Despair over the earthly or over something earthly"; and the second (60–67) bears the title "Despair of the eternal or over oneself."

6. "When the world is taken away from the self and one despairs, the despair seems to come from outside, even though it always comes from the self" (62).

7. The assertion of its originality, which underlies *The Sickness unto Death* as a whole, is already inherent in the thesis: "To despair over oneself, in despair to will to be rid of oneself—this is the formula for all despair" (20).

8. According to him: "If . . . the self does not become itself, then it is in despair, whether it knows that or not" (60).

9. In the conclusion, I will shed light on the continuity behind the appearance of completely discontinuity.

10. For the relationship of doubt and despair in Kierkegaard, see Wolfgang Janke, "Verzweiflung. Kierkegaards Phänomenologie des subjectiven Geistes," in *Sein und Geschichtlichkeit*, Festschrift für K. H. Volkmann-Schluck (Frankfurt a.M., 1974), 103–113.

11. See Pap. IV B16. In *Either/Or*, the ethicist expresses the thought thus: "Despair is precisely a much deeper and more complete expression; its movement is much more encompassing than that of doubt. Despair is an expression of the total personality, doubt only of thought" (*E/O* II, 212). The thesis that doubt becomes despair through totalization is prefigured in the famous passage in the introduction of *The Phenomenology of Spirit*, where Hegel—in view of the fact that consciousness loses all truth—says that the pathway of doubt is "more precisely" the way of despair (trans. A. V. Miller (Oxford: Oxford University Press, 1977), 49).

12. See *Iambi et Elegi Graeci*, ed. M. L. West, vol. 1, Editito altera (Oxford, 1989), Theognidea, vv. 1135–1136, p. 228.

13. I am speaking here of *early* Hellenism. Whether Aristotle had in mind real despair is another question. Günter Figal seems to give a positive answer in "Die Freiheit der Verzweiflung und die Freiheit im Glauben," *Kierkegaardiana* 13 (1984): 16–17. However, it seems doubtful to me whether the passage Figal cites (*Nicomachean Ethics*, 1166b) is really talking about despair.

14. According to Kierkegaard, despair is generally and as such a "category of totality" (90). I come back to that in Section III.2.

15. While the title of the passage analyzed here is: "*In Despair Not to Will to Be Oneself: Despair in Weakness*" (49), the text itself says: "But the despair is essentially that of weakness, a suffering [*en Liden*]" (54).

16. In the passage quoted, Kierkegaard continues: "its form is: in despair not to will to be oneself" (54).

17. On the one hand, it says: "Now something *happens* that impinges (*upon* + *to* strike) upon this immediate self and makes it despair" (51); on the other hand, we read: "despair is only a suffering, a succumbing to the pressure of external factors" (51), "it would be something that happens to a man, something he suffers" (16). The difference is important for the concluding observation (see the last section of this study).

18. In what follows, I shall continue to insist on this originality. Among the few treatises that seek an access to despair independent of Kierkegaard, the only one to provide a preliminary work for the rehabilitation of original suffering is an older dissertation, cited in the First Study but otherwise hardly noticed in the critical literature, which originated from the circle of phenomenological psychology: Max Sack, *Die Verzweiflung* (Kallmünz, 1930). Sack distinguishes between a "despair over facts outside oneself" (28–63) and an "internalized despair" (64–97). On the basis that despair is initially "suffering," he seeks to determine the specific difference of "suffering in despair" (4–5, see 33). His thesis is: "The basic emotion of despair is the attitude that one could not take upon oneself a certain fact and bear it" (35). To be sure, Sack admits, "at the end of his own investigation [he had] fallen under the spell of the Dane" (132).

19. See Sack, loc. cit., 38.

20. Kierkegaard's talk of those "whom bitter experiences and dreadful decisions have assisted in becoming conscious as spirit" (26) can be seen as the *voluntary* admission that the so-called external occupies an essential significance at least as immediate cause.

21. "A young girl despairs of love, that is, she despairs over the loss of her beloved, over his death or his unfaithfulness to her" (20).

22. The evaluation of the love discussed here as self-love goes through his whole book *Works of Love*.

23. "For example, when the ambitious man whose slogan is 'Either Caesar or nothing' does not get to be Caesar, he despairs over it. But this also means something else: precisely because he did not get to be Caesar, he now cannot bear to be himself. Consequently he does not despair because he did not get to be Caesar but despairs over himself because he did not get to be Caesar" (19).

24. Bernhard Meerpohl affirms this subsumption in a thoroughly uncritical manner in *Die Verzweiflung als metaphysisches Phänomen in der Philosophie Sören Kierkegaards* (Würzburg, 1934), p. 79. The entire fourth chapter of his book, on "Die Formen und Stufen der Verz-

weiflung" (78–98), closely follows Kierkegaard's hierarchization without any critical distance.

25. Kierkegaard continues: "It is the beginning, or as the physician says of an illness, it has not yet declared itself" (19).

26. "Here there is no infinite consciousness of the self, of what despair is, or of the condition as one of despair" (50–51).

27. With his characterization of despair over something, Kierkegaard resorts to the first of two cases that have already been discussed: "The customary view . . . assumes that every man must himself know best whether he is in despair or not. Anyone who says he is in despair is regarded as being in despair, and anyone who thinks he is not is therefore regarded as not" (22–23; and see 55–56).

28. Right at the beginning of his text, Kierkegaard contrasts the person attentive to his despair with one who "speaks meaninglessly of it as of something that is happening to him" (14). Correspondingly, in our passage on the person despairing over something, he says: "So he despairs—that is, in a strange reversal and in complete mystification about himself, he calls it despairing" (51).

29. That Kierkegaard pursues his analysis of despair as the diagnosis of a sickness encumbers it with *two* problems. The first problem, which I can only refer to here, is inherent in the analogy of despair and sickness. To be sure, Kierkegaard primarily emphasizes the distinctions between a somatic or psychic sickness and despair as a sickness of the spirit. However, he does not sufficiently respect the limits of the possibility of drawing analogies. The second problem is the one we confront in the present context. It resides in the superiority that Kierkegaard claims for himself when he elevates himself as physician over the patient. "As a rule, a person is considered to be healthy when he himself does not say that he is sick, not to mention when he himself says that he is well. But the physician has a different view of sickness. Why? Because the physician has a defined and developed conception of what it is to be healthy and ascertains a man's condition accordingly" (23). This problem touches the nerve of the analysis since it challenges its negativistic method. If Kierkegaard had remained faithful to his negativistic method, he would have had to follow his model, the *Phenomenology of Spirit*, in this point, too. Just as Hegel ascends from natural consciousness, he would also have had to descend to the person in despair and take him by the hand from there.

30. Kierkegaard refers to despair over oneself when he says: "This despair is a significant step forward. If the former despair was *despair in weakness*, then this is *despair over his weakness*." (61).

31. The attribute "immediate" is to identify clearly that even the despair *over* one's weakness is also a despair *in* weakness, if only a mediated one. "Consequently, there is only a relative difference, namely, that the previous form has weakness's consciousness as its final consciousness, whereas here the consciousness does not stop with that but rises to a new consciousness—that of his weakness" (61). The immediate despair of weakness is one that is itself an expression of weakness. It is accompanied only by that consciousness without which no despair is even conceivable. By contrast, the person in his despair reflects—over his weakness—on his despair.

32. "Nevertheless, this despair is classified under the form: in despair not to will to be oneself. Like a father who disinherits a son, the self does not want to acknowledge itself after having been so weak" (62).

33. "If the despair is intensified, it becomes defiance, and it now becomes clear how much untruth there was in this whole matter of weakness" (66).

34. "The person in despair himself understands that it is weakness to make the earthly so important, that it is weakness to despair. But now, instead of definitely turning away from despair to faith and humbling himself under his weakness, he entrenches himself in despair and despairs over his weakness" (61).

35. "No despair is entirely free of defiance, indeed, the very phrase 'not to will to be' implies defiance" (49).

36. "On the other hand, even despair's most extreme defiance is never really free of some weakness" (49).

37. "To elucidate this kind of despair more precisely, it is best to distinguish between an acting and a self acted upon" (68).

38. "If the self in despair is *acted upon*, the despair is nevertheless: in despair to will to be oneself. Perhaps such an imaginatively constructing self, which in despair wills to be itself, encounters some difficulty or other while provisionally orienting itself to its concrete self, something the Christian world would call a cross, a basic defect, whatever it may be" (70).

39. "A self that in despair wills to be itself is pained in some distress or other that does not allow itself to be taken away from or separated from his concrete self" (72). That being pained in some distress is a suffering in despair I say naturally from the perspective of the transcending critique.

40. The suppression of suffering in despair, which grounds rebellious defiance, is especially disconcerting since it amounts to a kind of self-suppression. The prominent passage at the beginning of the second section of the book, where Kierkegaard focuses on himself, as "a

poet-existence verging on the religious," resorts to the distress, to the "fixed point where the self suffers" (77).

41. As far as I can tell, he never expresses it in this form. But more or less concealed, it lurks in many of his expressions. Also, note the remarkable equation of defiance with will. "What constituent, then, does Socrates lack for the defining of sin? It is the will, defiance" (90).

42. "When the world is taken away from the self and one despairs, the despair seems to come from the outside, even though it always comes from the self; but when the self despairs over its despair, this new despair comes from the self, indirectly-directly from the self, as a counter-pressure (reaction), and it thereby differs from defiance, which comes directly from the self" (62).

43. It is not by chance that Kierkegaard puts special emphasis on the active nature of despair in his comments on despair over one's own weakness. He bases his argument that this despair is significant progress vis-à-vis the immediate despair of weakness on that it is "not merely a suffering, but an act" (62). In defiance, then, "despair is conscious of itself as an act" (67).

44. While the treatise on anxiety also focuses on anxiety's pathological manifestations, as in the section on the "somatic-psychic" loss of freedom, *The Sickness unto Death* is conspicuously hesitant to make statements on the clinical aspects of despair. That can be explained by the tendency to sublate not to will to be oneself in despairingly to will to be oneself. For the role of despair in the genesis of pathological depressions, see Hubertus Tellenbach, *Melancholie*, 2nd ed. (Berlin, Heidelberg, and New York, 1974), esp. pp. 143–147.

45. This proposition is a paraphrase of the last paragraph of the section that treats despair over something earthly and of the first paragraph of the following section on despair of the eternal (60–61). Both paragraphs together form the climax of the text.

46. I shall return to this rich footnote (60–61).

47. "Is there then no essential difference between the two expressions used identically up to now: to despair over the earthly (the category of totality) and to despair over something earthly (the particular)? Indeed there is. When the self in imagination despairs over something of this world, its infinite passion changes this particular thing, this something, into the world in toto, that is, the category of totality inheres in and belongs to the despairing person" (60). With this comment about his previous use of the expressions, Kierkegaard refers to the title of the section: "Despair over the earthly or over something earthly." Only now do we hear that he understood "or" as *vel*. But instead of *vel*, there is now no *aut*. Only now is the "or" given its ex-

planatory function: we are to read the title so that despair over something earthly is *rather* despair over the earthly in toto.

48. Here, the view of death that Kierkegaard handed down to Heidegger appears: the alleged despair over the death of another cannot be serious despair because there can be seriousness only in relation to one's own death. See Michael Theunissen, *Der Begriff Ernst bei Søren Kierkegaard*, 3rd ed. (Freiburg-Munich, 1982), section on "Der Ernst des Todes."

49. Referring to the so-called despair of reflected immediacy, Kierkegaard emphasizes that it "can be brought on by one's capacity for reflection, so that despair, when it is present, is not merely suffering, a succumbing to the external circumstance, but is to a certain degree self-activity, an act" (54). Accordingly, Kierkegaard draws a parallel between the "intensification consisting in moving from being acted upon to conscious action" and the "intensification of the consciousness of the self" (99).

50. The section devoted to something earthly begins with the sentence: "This is pure immediacy or immediacy containing a quantitative reflection" (50). Here, in Kierkegaard's self-understanding, "or" is to be read as *aut*. For the distinction, see W. Janke, "Verzweiflung Kierkegaards Phänomenologie des subjectiven Geistes," loc. cit. (note 10), 106–107.

51. As he says in *The Concept of Anxiety*, as he thinks, against Hegel: "The immediate is not to be annulled, because it at no time exists" (*The Concept of Anxiety*, ed. and trans. Reidar Thomte (Princeton, N.J.: Princeton University Press, 1980), 35.

52. The passage (whose continuation is also relevant) begins with the words: "In itself, to lose the things of this world is not to despair; yet that is what he talks about, and this is what he calls despairing. In a certain sense, what he says is true, but not in the way he understands it; he is conversely situated (*bagvendt situeret*), and what he says must be interpreted conversely (*bagvendt*): he stands and points to what he calls despair, but is not despair, and in the meantime, sure enough, despair is right there behind him without his realizing it" (51–52). This figure of reversal is characteristic of Kierkegaard's way of dealing with the person in despair. Where he classifies himself as "a poet-existence verging on the religious," within the ranks of persons in despair, as it were, he describes a word from such a poet-existence as something that "like every word from a person in despair, is inversely (*bagvendt*) correct and consequently to be understood inversely (*omvendt*)" (78). In his own way, Kierkegaard belongs to the unmaskers around him and, after him, to Feuerbach, Marx, and Freud.

53. "If the despairing person is aware of his despair, as he thinks he is, and does not speak meaninglessly of it as of something that is happening to him [...] and now with all his power seeks to break the despair by himself and by himself alone—he is still in despair and with all his presumed efforts only works himself all the deeper into deeper despair" (14). Accordingly, he says of the active self of the person in defiant despair: "In so far as the self in its despairing striving to be itself works itself into the very opposite, it really becomes no self" (69). Like everything in *The Sickness unto Death*, this process is also "dialectic." Comparing the despair over one's own weakness with the immediate despair in weakness, Kierkegaard comments: "simply because this despair is more intensive, it is in a certain sense closer to salvation" (62). This holds for the whole process of despair. What grows, however, is the closeness to an indispensable salvation through God. Consequently, the dialectic is one of proximity and distance. See 67: "But just because it is despair through the aid of the eternal, in a certain sense it is very close to the truth; and just because it lies very close to the truth, it is infinitely far away."

54. See Hildegard Kraus, "Verzweiflung und Selbstsein. Zum Ersten Abschnitt der *Krankheit zum Tode*," *Kierkegaardiana* 13 (1984): 40. Kraus points out that the view of the ethicist that despair can be remedied by "self choice" was already rejected by Johannes Climacus (quoted from the *Abschliessenden unwissenschaftlichen Nachschrift* in W. Janke, loc. cit., 104–105). Quite incomprehensibly, B. Meerpohl levels the two approaches in *Die Verzweiflung als metaphysisches Phänomen*, loc. cit. (note 24), chapter VI. The sentence "According to Kierkegaard, despair can be overcome only—through despair" (Meerpohl, 130) is valid for the Ethicist, but not for Anti-Climacus.

55. "What, then, is there to do? I have only one answer: Despair, then!" (*E/O* II, 208).

56. "But I shout it to you not as a consolation, not as a state in which you are to remain, but as an act that takes all the power and earnestness and concentration of the soul" (*E/O* II, 208).

57. "Choose despair, then, because despair itself is a choice, because one can doubt without choosing it, but one cannot despair without choosing it" (*E/O* II, 211).

58. That can also be seen in his language. He assures the addressee of his letter that "I" am "an upright married man, although I, too, *have* despaired (*har fortvivelt*)" (*E/O* II, 208, emphasis M.T.). E. Hirsch comments on that: "The version appropriate to the German language would be 'have been despaired.' But here and in the following, Kierkegaard means despair as a free active act. Thus we must take the risk

of the mistaken form 'have despaired' (p. 436 of the Diederichs Verlag edition). It is not that the prevailing laws of tense formation in Danish forced the Ethicist to use the active form. Indeed, "have despaired" is closer to the Danish in that one uses in that language the auxiliary verb *have*, unlike German, in conjunction with *vaere* (be). For "I *have* been despaired," the Dane says, "jeg *har* vaeret fortvivlet," and for "I *had* been despaired," he says, "jeg *havde* vaeret fortvivlet." But the Ethicist does not combine "have" with "been." He thinks "I have *de*spaired" may form an analogy with "I have doubted." If I am correct, such past forms no longer appear in *The Sickness unto Death*. This is probably not only due to the general effort of the author to say everything in a "linguistically correct" form (60n). Anti-Climacus also seems to draw a conclusion from the insight that despair has a past that cannot be traced back to any previous act (see IV.4).

59. The motif of a loss that is not a loss of self is discernible previously only in the context resorted to in the section that discusses the difference between despair over something and despair over oneself.

60. "to despair is to lose the eternal" (51).

61. "Despair over the earthly or over something earthly is in reality also despair of the eternal" (60).

62. "for the fact that he attributes such great worth to something earthly—or to carry this further, that he attributes to something earthly such great worth, or that he first makes something earthly into the whole world and then attributes such great worth to the earthly—this is in fact to despair of the eternal" (61).

63. See Johannes Sløk, *Die Anthropologie Kierkegaards* (Copenhagen, 1954), 62.

64. See the commentary of E. Hirsch here (p. 173 of the edition of Diedrich Verlag).

65. For J. Sløk, loc. cit., 62, the change of the preposition is "not only a linguistic finesse, but is of crucial significance."

66. Kierkegaard later changes the initial formulation, "to despair means to lose the eternal" to: "the loss of the eternal and of oneself" (62). The change should probably be seen as a certain correction. It applies not only to the person despairing over his weakness, "that he *has* lost the eternal and himself" (61, emphasis M.T.).

67. Someone who despairs over something "has been in despair his whole life" (24).

68. In this point, Anti-Climacus joins the author of the two volumes of *Either/Or*, who already says of the persons living aesthetically: "Consequently, when they despair, the basis of it must be that they were in

despair beforehand. The difference is only that they did not know it, but this is indeed an entirely accidental difference" (*E/O* II, 192).

69. The first time in the section on the universality of the sickness unto death: "As soon as despair becomes apparent, it is manifest that the individual was in despair" (24). See pp. 41–42.

70. He does this not only in the title of the section, "Despair of the eternal or over oneself," but also repeatedly later in the text. See, e.g., 67: "First comes despair over the earthly or over something earthly, then despair of the eternal, over oneself." Actually, from his insight that despair over ... is based on despair of ..., Kierkegaard would have to draw the conclusion that despair over oneself cannot coincide with despair of the eternal, either. When he says that despair "according to the concept, is always itself *of* the eternal, whereas *that which* is despaired *over* can be very diverse" (60n), he in fact degrades despair over oneself to one case among others of despair over.

71. See note 30.

72. See M. Theunissen, *Das Selbst auf dem Grund der Verzweiflung* (Frankfurt a.M., 1991), 41–42.

73. See B. Meerpohl, *Die Verzweiflung als metaphysisches Phänomen in der Philosophie Sören Kierkegaards*, loc. cit. (note 24), esp. chapter V (99–129). According to Meerpohl, Kierkegaard does not *describe* despair, he *defines* it, "namely by seeking to fathom the metaphysical event that takes place in and behind all despair in the depths of the human being" (100).

74. That is, the eternal in the proposition: "A human being is a synthesis of the infinite and finite, of the temporal and the eternal, of freedom and necessity. In short a synthesis" (13). For the synthesis of the temporal and the eternal, see Jann Holl, *Kierkegaards Konzeption des Selbes* (Meisenheim am Glan, 1972), 134.

75. Kierkegaard speaks of the fact that "there may even be something eternal in the self" (55) and that "consciousness of the eternal in the self breaks through" (60), in the passage on the despair in weakness that is of special interest here. By contrast, at the beginning it reads: "If a person were to die of despair as one dies of a sickness, then the eternal in him, the self, must be able to die in the same sense as the body dies of a sickness" (18). How fuzzy this concept of the eternal is, is revealed by the statement in parentheses: "next to God there is nothing as eternal as a self" (53), which tries to make one believe there are things that are more or less eternal.

76. In the circle of Kierkegaard interpreters, such a "deconstruction" is apparently deemed unnecessary. Basically, the critical literature has not gotten beyond paraphrases such as that a person despairs of

his "God-given, eternal fundamental nature" (Gerda Walther, "Sören Kierkegaards Psychologie der Verzweiflung," *Zeitschrift für Menschenkunde* 4 [1928]: 216; or that a person in despair does not believe "in the meaning of his spiritual nature reaching beyond everything earthly" (B. Meerpohl, *Die Verzweiflung als metaphysisches Phänomen*, 88).

77. "In the preceding pages, the form of despair that despairs over the earthly or something earthly was understood basically to be—and it also manifests itself as being—despair of the eternal, that is, an unwillingness to be comforted by and healed by the eternal, an overestimation of the things of this world to the extent that the eternal can be no consolation" (70).

78. "We despair *over* that which binds us in despair—over a misfortune, over the earthly, over a capital loss, etc.—but we despair *of* that which, rightly understood, releases us from despair: of the eternal, of salvation (*Frelse*), of our own strength, etc." (60–61n).

79. "And the haziness, particularly in all the lower forms of despair and in almost every person in despair, is that he so passionately and clearly sees and knows *over* what he despairs, but *of* what he despairs evades him" (61n).

80. "To understand that humanly it is his downfall and nevertheless to believe in possibility is to believe" (39).

81. "At this point, then salvation (*Frelse*) is, humanly speaking, utterly impossible; but for God everything is possible! This is the battle of *faith*, battling, madly, if you will, for possibility, because possibility is the only salvation. When someone faints, we call for water, eau de Cologne, smelling salts; but when someone wants to despair, then the word is: Get possibility, get possibility, possibility is the only salvation. A possibility—then the person in despair breathes again, he revives again, for without possibility a person seems unable to breathe" (38–39).

82. The fact that the passion with which the self makes his torment the object of all his passion becomes a "demonic rage" means: "even if God in heaven and all the angels offered to help him out of it—no, he does not want that [. . .] What demonic madness—the thought that most infuriates him is that eternity could get the notion to deprive him of his misery" (72).

83. See M. Theunissen, "'Ο αἰτῶν λαμβάνει. Der Gebetsglaube Jesu und die Zeitlichkeit des Christseins," in *Negative Theologie der Zeit*, 2nd ed. (Frankfurt a.M, 1992), 321–377. For Kierkegaard, see the section, "Glaube und Selbstsein" (339–355).

84. "Since everything is possible for God, then God is this—that everything is possible. [. . .] the being of God means that everything is possible, or that everything is possible means the being of God" (40).

85. The person despairing in rebellious defiance rejects not only the "humiliation" that help from "a superior, or by the supreme one" means for him; he cannot even bear "simply having to yield to another person, of giving up being himself as long as he is seeking help" (71). The self-enclosed person, whom a person despairing over his weakness ultimately becomes, can be saved by another person at least insofar as communication prevents him from committing suicide (65–67). However, it is characteristic of Kierkegaard that he immediately points out the danger lurking here: "However, it may happen that just because he has opened himself to another person he will despair over having done so; it may seem to him that he might have held out far far longer in silence rather than to have a confidant" (66).

86. See Helmut Fahrenbach, *Kierkegaards existenzdialektische Ethik* (Frankfurt a.M., 1968), 33, where the "absolute ground" is defined more completely as that "through which," "whereof," and "that in the face of which" the self exists.

87. At the beginning is: "the formula that describes the state of the self when despair is completely rooted out is this: in relating itself to itself and in willing to be itself, the self rests transparently in the power that established it" (14). The concluding sentence of the book refers back to it: "This formula in turn, as has been frequently pointed out, is the definition of faith" (131). Kierkegaard calls this formula "the definition of faith, by which I steer in this whole book as a trustworthy navigation guide" (82).

88. See M. Theunissen, *Das Selbst auf dem Grund der Verzweiflung*, loc. cit. (note 72), 61ff.

89. Kierkegaard's attempt to distinguish accepting from enduring is also shown by the fact that, after declaring in *Fear and Trembling* the "infinite resignation" to the precondition of faith, he considers in *The Sickness unto Death* resignation—or rather "much of what in the world is dressed up under the name of resignation"—as a form of despair (70n). Accepting must not be an enduring of "the earthly and the temporal," which, to make up for the suffering in that, finds consolation in the idea of a future eternity. At this point, it would also have to be interpreted in full that Kierkegaard explicates both the active and the suffering form of defiance in terms of the common denominator of "stoicism" (68). But he hardly makes his right for doing so plausible, so that referring to that circumstance as such must suffice. See W. Janke, "Verzweiflung," loc. cit. (note 10). 111.

90. An interesting attempt to define belief from freedom as "a movement of freedom beyond being" is undertaken by Günter Figal, "Die Freiheit der Verzweiflung und die Freiheit im Glauben," loc. cit.

(note 13), 11–23, esp. 20ff. And see Torsten Bohlin, "Angst, Verzweiflung und Glaube. Ein Beitrag zum Verständnis der Sündenauffassung bei Kierkegaard," in *Glaube und Ethos*, Festschrift for D. Wehrung (Stuttgart n.d.), 143.

91. "Thus possibility seems greater and greater to the self, more and more becomes possible because nothing becomes actual. Eventually everything seems possible, but this is exactly the point at which the abyss swallows up the self" (39). "In possibility everything is possible" (37).

92. Thus Kierkegaard on the person who withstands the "struggle of faith": "Whether or not the embattled one collapses depends solely upon whether he obtains possibility, that is, whether he will believe. And yet he understands that, humanly speaking, his collapse is altogether certain" (39). "Whether a person is helped miraculously depends essentially upon the passion of the understanding whereby he has understood that help was impossible and depends next on how honest he was toward the power that nevertheless did help him" (39).

93. "What is missing is essentially the power to obey, to submit to the necessity in one's life, to what might be called one's limitations" (36).

94. See M. Theunissen, *Das Selbst auf dem Grund der Verzweiflung*, loc. cit. (note 72), 40ff. I am trying to show here that this synthesis is nonetheless always present to the author.

95. This pertains primarily to the section on the person who lacks infinitude: "Just by losing himself this way, such a man has gained an increasing capacity for going along superbly in business and social life, indeed, for making a great success in the world" (34).

96. The concluding sentence of the text on despair as a deficiency of the synthesis is: "The person who gets lost in possibility soars high with the boldness of despair; he for whom everything became necessary overstrains himself in life and is crushed in despair; but the philistine-bourgeois mentality spiritlessly triumphs" (42). Herein lies a partial admission concerning the form of finitude, of the non-despaired nature of finitude or infinitude made absolute. With the expression "philistine-bourgeois mentality," Kierkegaard does resort to a special form of despair defined as totalization of necessity, which he differentiates into determinism or fatalism or philistine-bourgeois mentality. But his discussion of this in turn takes up comments on the despair of finitude. He knows no other way than to reduce the despair of finitude to the level of inauthentic despair. "The despair that not only does not cause one any inconvenience in life, but makes life cozy and comfortable, is in no way, of course, regarded as despair" (34). Here, Kierke-

gaard describes the despair of finitude as he had previously described proper inauthentic despair: as a real despair which, however, is not regarded as such.

97. For the problem of the content of despair of different types of a failing synthesis, see Hildegard Kraus, "Verzweiflung und Selbstsein," loc. cit. (note 54), 44–45. Kraus believes it may be said of all types that they were "strictly speaking not yet forms of despair." The same holds for Max Sack, *Die Verzweiflung*, loc. cit. (note 18), 133ff.

98. The distinction between an acting and a suffering self is already hinted at in those passages that correspond structurally to the passage about the despair of defiance, in the sections on the despair of infinitude and of possibility. In the section on the former, Kierkegaard distinguishes between a "more active" and a "more passive" form of becoming fantastic, as which he interprets this despair (32); and in the section on the latter, he takes up this distinction in the form that he differentiates the self's running away from itself into a "despairing, craving" and a "melancholic-imaginary" form (37).

99. Kierkegaard discusses a kind of suffering in the context of his description of the "melancholic-imaginary" form that he characterizes as "fear or anxiety." By referring to anxiety, he seems to aim at the feeling of emptiness. After all, he originally conceives of anxiety as anxiety of indeterminateness. But at the same time, he sees in it a "sympathetic antipathy and an antipathetic sympathy" (VI 313). Thus, with anxiety, not only a repulsion comes into play, but also an attraction. "Melancholically enamored, the individual pursues one of anxiety's possibilities, which finally leads him away from himself so that he is a victim of anxiety or a victim of that about which he was anxious lest he overcome" (37). There is nothing corresponding to such a love in fully developed despair. The suspicion that the despair of possibility is not yet a despair in the full sense is also fueled by the circumstance that Kierkegaard appeals to anxiety at all. Anxiety here seems to play a substitutive function similar to the one it has in the context of his attempt to demonstrate the universality of unconscious despair by way of its construct.

100. That Kierkegaard himself suspected that can perhaps be inferred from what he says about possibility: "If this is lacking, if a human existence is brought to the point where it lacks possibility, then it is in despair and is in despair every moment it lacks possibility" (37). This is also reminiscent of the concluding sentence of the analysis of deficiency, that only the one for whom everything has become necessary is "de-pressed" in despair. The opposition of extravagance and despondency prefigures the distinction of mania and depression.

101. "But this is also a form of despair, to be unwilling to hope in the possibility that an earthly need, a temporal cross, can come to an end" (70).

102. That doubt is limited to the cognitive sphere, whereas despair extends to the whole of existence, is already suggested by the Ethicist in *Either/Or*: "Doubt is thought's despair, despair is personality's doubt" (*E/O* II, 211).

103. *Summa theologiae* II/2, quaestio 20, art. 4.

104. Cornelio Fabro points to other sources in the traditional theology of sin, "The Problem of Desperation and Christian Spirituality in Kierkegaard," *Kierkegaardiana* 4 (1962): 63–69.

105. *Summa theologiae* II/2, qu. 20, a.I, ad primum: *peccata quae opponuntur virtutibus theologicis, ut odium Dei, et desperatio, et infidelitas* [the sins which are contrary to the theological virtues, such as hatred of God, despair and unbelief].

106. *Summa theologiae* II/2, qu. 20, a.3.

107. According to Thomas, despair can break out *ex horrore propriorum peccatorum* [of the horror of one's own sins] (qu. 20, a. I, *ad secundum*).

108. *Summa theologiae* II/2, qu. 20, a. 2: *Respondeo dicendum quod infidelitas pertinet ad intellectum, desperatio autem ad vim appetitivam* [I answer that, unbelief pertains to the intellect, but despair, to the appetite].

109. See Raymond Klibansky, Erwin Panofsky, and Fritz Saxl, *Saturn and Melancholy: Studies in the History of Natural Philosophy, Religion and Art* (New York, 1964).

110. *Summa theologiae* II/2, qu. 20, a. 2.

111. Aquinas devotes to the *praesumptio* the whole *quaestio* 21 of his theological *Summa*. For the reference to hope, see esp. a.I: *Respondeo dicendum quod praesumptio videtur importare quamdam immoderantiam spei* [I answer that, Presumption seems to imply immoderate hope].

112. Thomas in the *Summa theologiae*, qu. 21, a. 4.

113. "Possibility and necessity belong to the self as do infinitude and finitude (απειρον—περας)" (35).

114. In his attempt to demonstrate the defiance in the despair in weakness through its reflective form, he explicitly appeals to pride. It says of the self-enclosed person: "If it were possible for anyone to share the secret of his enclosing reserve and if one were then to say to him, 'It is pride, you are really proud of yourself,' he probably would never make the confession to anyone else. Alone with himself, he no doubt would confess that there is something to it, but the passionateness with which his self has interpreted his weakness would soon lead him into believing that it cannot possibly be pride, because it is indeed his very

weakness that he despairs over—just as if it were not pride that places such tremendous emphasis on weakness, just as if it were not because he wants to be proud of his self that he cannot bear this consciousness of weakness" (65).

115. For the reference to Goethe of our book, see Georg Siegmund, "Die Krankheit zum Tode. Goethe—Kierkegaard," *Hochland* 53 (1961): 534–542; Carl Roos, *Kierkegaard og Goethe* (Copenhagen, 1955), esp. 56–157.

116. "The devil's despair is the most intensive despair, for the devil is sheer spirit and hence unqualified consciousness and transparency; there is no obscurity in the devil that could serve as a mitigating excuse. Therefore, his despair is the most absolute defiance. This is despair at its maximum" (42).

117. Only in this sense can it be said that the forms considered in terms of the synthesis and the forms considered in terms of consciousness "in fact coincide objectively and substantively" (B. Meerpohl, *Die Verzweiflung als metaphysisches Phänomen*, loc. cit., 123).

118. On this point, I differ with M. Sack, who devotes a separate section of his book to the relation between despair and hopelessness (*Die Verzweiflung*, loc. cit., 15–27).

119. "Interpreted this way, Mephistopheles (in *Faust*) quite properly says that nothing is more miserable than a devil who despairs, for here despair must be interpreted as a willingness to be weak enough to hear something about repentance and grace" (109). Kierkegaard refers to the concluding words of the scene, "Forest and Cave."

120. See M. Theunissen, *Das Selbst auf dem Grund der Verzweiflung*, loc. cit., II.2.2, "Der Mensch als Synthese gegensätzlicher Momente" (38–51); M. Theunissen, "Das Menschenbild in der *Krankheit zum Tode*," in M. Theunissen and W. Greve, *Materialien zur Philosophie Søren Kierkegaards* (Frankfurt a.M., 1979), 496–509, esp. 500ff.

121. "The youth despairs over the future, as the present *in futuro*; there is something in the future that he is not willing to take upon himself, and therefore he does not will to be himself. The adult despairs over the past as a present *in praeterito* that refuses to recede further into the past, for his despair is not such that he has even succeeded in forgetting it completely" (59). The Danish editor refers the grammatical terms to the objects of despair. E. Hirsch refers them to the despairing persons (edition of Diederichs Verlag, p. 173). Hirsch's critique of the Danish editors is unjustified on this point. Kierkegaard does indeed conceive of the future and the past as being in the present. Only that critique of the critique is correct which A. B. Drachmann, J. L. Heiberg, and H. O. Lange exercise by claiming that the grammat-

ical terms do not correspond with what is meant. Being in the present is a necessary condition for the fact that men are able to despair over the future and the past. The future is present to the youth as something he does not want to accept in his self-being; the past is present to the adult as something he cannot "get done with" in Erwin Straus's sense. For this, see M. Theunissen, "Melancholisches Leiden unter der Herrschaft der Zeit," in *Negative Theologie der Zeit*, loc. cit. (note 83), 218–281, esp. 5, section on "Nicht-erledigen-Können" (251ff.). In the case of the future, consideration of the reference to the present is especially important because it is what really allows the author to speak of a despair *over*.

122. *Summa theologiae* II/2, qu. 20. a. I, ad tertium: *si medicus desperet de curatione alicujus informi* [if a physician were to despair of curing some sick man]. Another example, however, raises the question of whether Aquinas even distinguishes despair of from despair over. In the context of the quotation, it says: *sicut etiam in statu viae si quis desperaret de eo quod non est natus adipisci, non esset peccatum* [Even so, it would be no sin if a traveler despaired of obtaining that which he had no natural capacity for obtaining]. The person really despairs *over* what he cannot obtain. A despair analogous to *desperatio de curatione* [despair of curing] would be a despair of the ability to obtain.

123. The "objective" anxiety (*CA*, 56–60) is even one that has accumulated in the past, in the whole previous history of mankind. But for the very same reason, anxiety here does not *refer* to the past. The "subjective" anxiety (*CA*, 60–80), that which is "established in the individual," remains related to the future, too. Melancholy is already oriented to the future inasmuch as it takes hold of a person at the moment of the development of his personality, at which he is to seize himself, that is, to project himself in the future. See the paradigm of Nero in volume 2 of *Either/Or* (*E/O* II, 184ff.) and *E/O* II, 349.

Summarizing Conclusion: Dialectic in *The Sickness unto Death*

1. Gerda Walther, "Sören Kierkegaards Psychologie der Verzweiflung," *Zeitschrift für Menschenkunde* 4 (1928): 208.
2. In a journal entry of May 13, 1848, titled "Report on 'The Sickness unto Death'" (Pap. VIII, A 651). The note is conveyed, like the following, in the "Historical Introduction" to *The Sickness unto Death*, ed. and trans. Howard V. Hong and Edna H. Hong (Princeton, N.J.: Princeton University Press, 1980), p. xiv.

3. Pap. VIII, A 652.
4. Pap. VIII, A 651.
5. For the dialectical method of securing presuppositions, see Rüdiger Bubner, *Dialektik und Wissenschaft* (Frankfurt a.M., 1973).
6. See Michael Theunissen, *Das Selbst auf dem Grund der Verzweiflung Kierkegaards negativistische Methode* (Frankfurt a.M., 1991).
7. "In the relation between two, the relation is the third as a negative unity, and the two relate to the relation and in the relation to the relation; thus, under the qualification of the psychical the relation between the psychical and the physical is a relation. If, however, the relation relates itself to itself, this relation is the positive third, and this is the self" (13).
8. "Consequently, the progress of the becoming must be an infinite moving away from itself in the infinitizing (*Uendeliggjørelse*) of the self, and in infinite coming back to itself in the finitizing process (*Endeliggjørelse*)" (30). Kierkegaard explains this dialectic in the section on the despair of infinitude: "The self is likewise gradually volatilized when will becomes fantastic. Willing, then, does not continually become proportionately as concrete as it is abstract, so that the more infinite it becomes in purpose and determination, the more personally present and contemporary it becomes in the small part of the task that can be carried out at once, so that in being infinitized it comes back to itself in the most rigorous sense, so that when furthest away from itself (when it is most infinite in purpose and determination), it is simultaneously and personally closest to carrying out the infinitely small part of the work that can be accomplished this very day, this very hour, this very moment" (31–32). I have been repeatedly concerned with this double movement ever since my dissertation (1955). See esp. M. Theunissen, "'Ο ἡ αἰτῶν λαμβάνει," in *Negative Theologie der Zeit*, 2nd ed. (Frankfurt a.M., 2nd ed., 1992), 345ff.
9. Pp. 30 and 33. Hirsch translates: "and therefore each constituent is what is opposite to itself" (pp. 26 and 29 of Diederichs edition). This is linguistically correct, but misleading. For it invites association with Hegel's thought of the other of itself, which was far from what Kierkegaard had in mind. Kierkegaard means exclusively that each constituent is its opposite, that is, the other that it is not.
10. The text about the despair of possibility also repeats the sentence in an abbreviated form (35).
11. In the text about the despair of infinitude, Kierkegaard continues: "No form of despair can be *defined* directly (that is, undialectically), but only by reflecting on its opposite. The condition of the person in despair can be *described* directly, as the poet in fact does by

giving him lines to speak. But the despair can be *defined* only by way of its opposite, and if the lines are to have any poetic value, the coloring of the expression must contain the reflection of the dialectical opposite" (30, emphases M.T.).

12. "Good health generally means the ability to resolve contradictions" (40).

13. *Hegel's Science of Logic*, trans. A. V. Miller, foreword by J. N. Findlay (New York: Prometheus, 1999), p. 440.

14. "This is the good health of faith that resolves contradictions" (40).

15. For the section, "Contradiction resolves itself" and for Hegel's theory of determinations of reflection in general, see M. Theunissen, "Krise der Macht. Thesen zur Theorie des dialektischen Widerspruchs," in *Hegel-Jahrbuch 1974* (Cologne, 1975), 318–329, esp. 323.

16. See Wolfgang Janke, "Verzweiflung Kierkegaards Phänomenologie des subjektiven Geistes," in *Sein und Geschichtlichkeit*, Festschrift for K.-H. Volkmann-Schluck (Frankfurt a.M., 1974), 103–113.

17. Introduction to Hegel's *Phenomenology of* Spirit, trans. A. V. Miller (Oxford: Oxford University Press, 1977), p. 49 (see note 11 of the Second Study).

18. See note 57 of the First Study. The formulation of the general principle is preceded by the following propositions: "Compared with the person who is conscious of his despair, the despairing individual who is ignorant of his despair is simply a negativity further away from the truth and deliverance. Despair itself is a negativity; ignorance of it, a new negativity" (44). Subsuming the despair in which the person is ignorant of being in despair under the concept of negativity makes clear that the unconsciousness is part of the appearance that must dissolve itself in the process of maximization.

19. See *Das Selbst auf dem Grund der Verzweiflung*, loc. cit. (note 6), esp. 24ff.

20. Karl Marx and Friedrich Engels, *Werke* (Berlin, 1971), vol. 23, p. 27; *The Collected Works of Karl Marx and Frederick Engels* (New York: International, 1975—), vol. 35, p. 19.

21. See the second part of my article, "Krise der Macht," loc. cit. (note 15).

22. "Meanwhile, time passes. If help arrives from the outside, the person in despair comes alive again, he begins where he left off, a self he was not, and a self he did not become, but he goes on living, qualified *only by immediacy*. If there is no external help, something else frequently happens in actual life. In spite of everything, there is still life in the person, but he says that 'he will never be himself again.' He now acquires a little understanding of life, he learns to copy others, how

they manage their lives—and he now proceeds to live the same way" (52, emphasis—M.T.). Elsewhere, Kierkegaard treats the heteronomous ideas of value of such a form of life, which is considered as a despair of finitude in *The Sickness unto Death*, under the title of a "finite ethics," which expresses well the reflection, itself finite, that is contained in immediacy.

23. Here I should point to the proposition quoted in note 34 of the Second Study, that the person who despairs over his weakness entrenches himself in his despair "instead of definitely turning away from despair to faith" (61). In this turning away, Kierkegaard sees so little of a possibility open to the person in despair that he does not even consider whether, aside from the despair over one's weakness, there is also a non-despaired reflection on this weakness. The reference to the failed alternative of turning away is what Hegel would call an "external reflection"; the reference is made not from the perspective of the person affected, but from Kierkegaard's perspective of observation. This becomes even clearer somewhat later: "You are quite right about the weakness, but that is not what you are to despair over; the self must be broken in order to become itself, but quit despairing over that" (65). Kierkegaard brings this demand to the person in despair from outside; he confronts him with an "Ought" that is alien to him.

24. It is generally not sufficiently considered that in the books following the *Concluding Unscientific Postscript*, his critique of Hegel recedes drastically. On occasion, Kierkegaard can even call Hegel a master in his journals of the late '40s. What remains valid, of course, is the genuinely existential critique of the system builder, who himself personally lives not in the palace he erected, but in a doghouse (43–44). The polemic writings of the '50s and the journals of these years, however, degenerate into an extreme hyper-Platonic dualism, which no longer shows any proximity to Hegel, not even the proximity of a critique. The reason for that is probably not only his attack on the Church, but also a break with the endeavors of thought documented in *The Sickness unto Death*—a break whose motives are also seldom considered.

25. See notes 27 and 60 of the First Study.

Index

accepting oneself, self-acceptance, 22, 29, 85
acedia, 93–94
act, totalizing, 64, 67–69
acting: self-activity, 60–72, 89–90; transformation of suffering into activity, 114; unity of acting and suffering, 69–71, 90
Adorno, Theodor Wiesengrund, 132n.73
anxiety (fear), 8, 75, 93, 99–100, 126–127n.37, 147n.99, 150n.123
Aquinas, Thomas, 93–95, 98, 100; *Summa theologiae*, 148nn.103, 105–108, and 110–112
Aristotle, 24, 94; *Nicomachean Ethics*, 130n.58, 135n.13
asymmetry, 62; of in despair to will and not to will to be oneself, 13, 34, 111; of weakness and defiance, 58–59, 111

bad faith (*mauvaise foi*), 30–31
being human, 4, 6–8, 14, 16, 20, 22, 25, 107–108
Bohlin, Torsten, 146n.90
Borgia, Cesare, 50–52

contradiction, 113, 115–116, 125n.26, 126n.34
critique, immanent/transcending, 3, 35–42, 44–45, 69–70, 111, 117; transcending, 47–48, 61, 79

Dasein, 11, 125–126n.30; imaginary/factual, 12; individual, 25; pre-given, 6–9, 12, 14–15, 20, 22, 118, 130n.60
defiance, 12, 53–62, 66, 69, 82, 90, 96–97, 99–100, 111; active/passive (suffering) form of, 145n.89; in the arrogance of self-construction, 13, 16, 54; as principle of self-activity, 60; rebellious, 13–14, 16, 22, 54, 57–58, 82, 125–126n.30; of rejection/of acceptance, 59; three kinds of, 13–14; in weakness, 58–59; of willing the impossible, 14, 16, 54, 60
definition of man, 24–25, 43–44
depression/mania, 101, 147n.100
despair: as act, 61–62; active/passive, 89; all or every
despair, 39, 61, 69, 72, 76–77; authentic, 9–10, 12, 14–16, 40, 76; authentic/inauthentic, 9–10, 34,

despair (*cont.*)
39, 41, 51; consideration of: synthetic-theoretical/in terms of a theory of consciousness, 16–17, 97; of defiance, 58, 96–97; demonic, 82, 126n.33; not being in despair, 9, 21–22, 29; not being in despair: perversion of, 35, 126n.33; and doubt (relation to doubt), 46–47; of the eternal, 72–73, 76, 79, 81, 99, 103–104; as event happening to oneself, 49, 51, 67, 104, 114, 117–118; of finitude/of infinitude, 88, 92, 108–111, 146–147n.96; forms of, 17–18, 110; formula for all despair, 20–21; over the future/over the past, 100; historicity of, 45; inauthentic, 14–16, 28, 51, 68, 146–147n.96; interpretation of (disclosing/closing off), 37–38, 41, 44–45, 112; as loss, 71–73; in the meaning of the German and Danish word (*fortvivelse*), 45–46, 92, 98; of necessity, 89–91, 97; of necessity and finitude, 27–28; over oneself, 21, 40, 52–53, 67, 76; originality of, 48–49, 57; *over/of*, 63, 75, 79–80, 100–102, 143n.70; past of, 101–103, 141–142n.58; phenomenology of, 36, 77–78; of possibility, 89–91, 97; of possibility/of necessity, 18, 86–89; progressive/regressive movement of, 116; of the self-relation, 76; over something, 49, 51, 65–69, 75–77, 101–103; over something/over oneself, 17, 37, 50–51, 67–68, 72, 103–104; over something earthly, 67; over something earthly/over the earthly in toto, 69; over something earthly (the earthly)/of the eternal, 63–64, 73–75, 102, 128n.43; of that which saves, 81; as totalizing doubt, 92; true/seeming, 103; universality of, 28, 126–127n.37; in weakness, 48–49, 54, 77, 96–97, 139n.41; in weakness/of defiance, 12, 13, 47–48, 56, 61, 128–129n.44, 130n.60, 134n.3; in weakness/over one's weakness, 52–53; over one's weakness, 53–54, 56, 62, 77, 79, 128n.43, 139n.41, 153n.23; of to will to be oneself/not to will to be oneself, 9–10, 17, 27, 34, 50

desperatio, 45–47, 91–100, 102–103
desperation: of an act, 60–61, 98; of the self-relation, 41
despondency, 98, 100
determinateness, 25; determinateness/indeterminateness, 7 dialectic, 5, 105–119, 127n.38, 141n.53; of in despair to will and not to will to be oneself, 63; dichotomous/trichotomous, 111; existential, 3–4, 106; phenomenological, 114, 117; positive, 108; "real" dialectic, 106; speculative, 114–115; synthetic, 111
doubt, 46–47, 91–92, 94

earthly, the: distinction between something earthly and the earthly as such, 64–65; opposition of the earthly and the eternal, 78
establishing, or grounding, oneself (in God), 22, 84
eternal, the, 73, 75, 78–86, 125n.26
existentiality, 26
existentiell (-ontic) / existential (-ontological), 4, 10, 26–27, 30

facticity, 7, 26–27
faith, 31, 46–47, 81–84, 86–88, 90–91, 94, 99, 113, 117, 119, 122n.1
fear. *See* anxiety
Fichte, Johann Gottlieb, 2; *Vocation of Man*, 114
Figal, Günter, 135n.13, 145n.90
freedom, 31, 93, 115, 119
Freud, Sigmund, 140
fundamental principle (*Grundsatz*), 3–6, 8–9, 20, 22–23, 27, 34–35

God, 12, 82–87, 90
Goethe, Johann Wolfgang, 96, 149n.115; *Faust*, 96, 149n.119
Greve, Wilfried, 123n.9

Habermas, Jürgen, *Philosophical Discourse of Modernity*, 133n.77
Hannay, Alastair, 121n.6
Hartmann, Nicolai, 106, 108
health, 112–113
Hegel, Georg Wilhelm Friedrich, 2, 7, 57, 66, 105–109, 112–118, 124n.16, 137n.29, 153nn.23 and 24; *Phenomenology of Spirit*, 114–115; 152n.17; *Science of Logic*, 152n.13
Heidegger, Martin, 4, 132nn.69 and 73, 133nn.77 and 78; *Being and Time*, 26–30, 130–131n.63, 132nn.64, 65, 67, 70, and 72, 133nn.74–76
Hirsch, E., 141n.58, 142n.64, 149n.121, 151n.9
history, historical, 7, 44–47, 116
Hohlenberg, Johannes, 122n.3
Holl, Jann, 143
hope (*spes*), 46, 94–95
hopelessness, abandonment or loss of hope, 46, 91, 94–95, 97–99, 102–103, 126n.34

humility, self-humiliation, humbling oneself, 22, 25, 29, 55, 84, 87

immediacy: mediation of, 114; pure/with quantitative (finite) reflection in itself, 66–69, 117; seeming (appearance of), 115, 117
individuality, 24, 43–44

Janke, Wolfgang, 135n.10, 145n.89, 140n.50, 141n.54
Jaspers, Karl, 26; *Psychologie der Weltanschauungen*, 130n.60
Jonas, Hans, 132n.69

Kafka, Franz, 23
Kierkegaard, Søren Aabye, works of cited: *The Concept of Anxiety* (1844), 5, 25; *Either/Or* (1843 and 1849), 25, 36, 70–71, 85, 142–143n.68; *Fear and Trembling* (1843), 145n.89; *Works of Love* (1847), 136n.22
Klibansky, Raymond, 148n.109
Kraus, Hildegard, 127n.38, 141n.54, 147n.97,

loss, 49–50, 71, 75, 85–86; of the earthly, 86; of the earthly/of the eternal, 72, 76; of the eternal, 72–73, 77; of meaning, 24, 44, 86, 114; of that which saves, 81, 86; of trust, 99

Marx, Karl, 25, 115–116, 140n.52, 152n.20; *Das Kapital*, 115
Meerpohl, Bernhard, *Die Verzweiflung als metaphysisches Phänomen*, 123n.9, 136–137n.24, 141n.54, 143n.73, 144n.76, 149n.117
melancholy, 93–94, 150n.123

Mephistopheles (devil), 96, 98
metaphysics, 24, 77, 83, 86
method, 29, 106; dialectical, 106; negativistic, 22, 106, 137n.29; negativistic-dialectical, 107
modernity, 23, 93

negativism, negativistic, 29–30
negativity, 31, 114–115, 118, 130n.57
Nero, 150n.123
nihilism, 36, 43–45, 47, 85–86, 90

opposition: of in despair to will and not to will to be oneself, 110; of weakness and defiance, 53–56

Panofsky, Erwin, 148n.109
paradox, 113, 119
Plato, 24; Platonism, 77, 83, 85
Popper, Karl, 106
praesumptio, 94–100
premise(s), 39, 42, 107; anthropological, 4, 107; fundamental, 3–6, 8–9, 14–15, 20, 38; securing of, 115; as theological preliminary decisions, 3–6, 11, 107
presupposition(s). *See* premise(s)
pride (*superbia*), 95–97, 99
process, 17–18, 89, 92, 97, 108, 114, 118

reconstruction, 1–3, 8–9, 35, 123n.11
reducibility, of both forms of authentic despair to one another, 12–13, 34, 53–54, 59
reflection, 27, 66–69, 103–104, 131n.66; determinations of, 109, 111, 113, 116
resignation, 145n.89
revolt, 12, 14, 16–17, 35

Richardson, William J., 133n.78; *Heidegger: Through Phenomenology to Thought*, 130n.61
Roos, Carl, *Kierkegaard og Goethe*, 149n.115
rupture, 95–96, 98, 113

Sack, Max, *Die Verzweiflung*, 125n.30, 127nn.37 and 38, 136nn.18 and 19, 147n.97, 149n.118
Sartre, Jean-Paul, *Being and Nothingness*, 26, 29–33, 129n.48, 133n.79, 133–134n.80, 134nn.81–84
Saxl, Fritz, 148n.109
Schelling, Friedrich Wilhelm Joseph von, 2, 6, 123n.13
Schopenhauer, Arthur, 2
self, 4, 6–11, 14–16, 20–22, 25–27, 78–79, 83–84, 103, 108, 118, 131n.66; abstract (negative)/concrete, 7, 10; acting/acted upon (suffering), 56–57, 147n.98; as being established by God, 4, 6, 11, 26, 83–84, 87; hypothetical (constructed), 11, 131–132n.68; realization of (self-realization), 23–24; as relation, 4, 10–11, 15, 26–27, 39–41, 49–50, 59, 67, 79, 84, 104; as deficient relation, 88; self-relation of (despair as written into the self-relation), 39–41; negative self-relation of, 90; as source of despair, 39–41
sickness, 52, 63, 134n.84, 137n.29
Siegmund, Georg, 149n.115
sin, 5, 32, 36, 93–94, 123n.12
Sløk, Johannes, *Die Anthropologie Kierkegaards*, 142nn.63 and 65
Socrates, 123n.12, 139n.41
Straus, Erwin, 150n.121

suffering, 48, 61–63, 65–66, 70, 72–73, 89–90; movement from acting to being acted upon (suffering), 89
synthesis, 4, 6, 19, 78, 92, 99, 106, 113; deficiency or failure of, 16, 35, 41, 88, 99, 109

Tellenbach, Hubertus, *Melancholie*, 139n.44
that which saves, 79–86, 99
Theognis, 46, 135n.12
theology, 83, 94, 107
theory, self-transcending elements of, 37–38, 47–48, 59–60, 69–70, 81, 99
time, temporality, temporal structure of despair, 74, 99–100
totalization, 46–47, 64–65, 67, 114; of doubt, 46–47, 92, 98; negative, 89–91

Walther, Gerda, 143–144n.76, 150n.1

weakness, 54, 100, 111; in defiance, 58–59, 89; of suffering, 57–61, 94; of not to will to be oneself/of suffering, 48, 50–53, 56–57
will, 27, 131n.66, 139n.41
willing, 30, 43, 49; not to accept oneself, 8, 20, 22; to be, 27, 41, 43; not to be, 42, 55; in despair to be oneself, 10–11, 13–14, 22, 28, 34–35, 53, 55, 57, 59, 96, 100; to be oneself: legitimately so-called, 10–11, 13, 22, 28, 59; to be oneself: illegitimately so-called (willing to be what one is not), 10–11, 13, 100; to be oneself: as not being in despair, 25, 29, 43–44; to be oneself: as not willing to be oneself, 21; not to be oneself, 10–11, 13, 21, 27–28, 49–50, 52–56, 100, 103; to get rid of oneself, 8, 20, 22; not willing, 16, 35; willing the impossible, 14, 21, 25, 32–33, 39, 41, 55

GPSR Authorized Representative: Easy Access System Europe - Mustamäe tee
50, 10621 Tallinn, Estonia, gpsr.requests@easproject.com

www.ingramcontent.com/pod-product-compliance
Lightning Source LLC
Chambersburg PA
CBHW030625230426
43661CB00053B/2147